THE WALKING UNCONSCIOUS

Henrique Guilherme Scatolin

2nd Edition

GlobalSouth
P R E S S

For more information, please contact
info@globalsouthpress.com or go to
http://www.globalsouthpress.com/

The Walking Unconscious

By SCATOLIN, Henrique—2nd ed. — 2016
1st Edition Published by David Publishing LLC
Includes bibliographical references and index.
ISBN: 978-1541169432

1. Psicology — Freudian Theory

2. Psicology — Contemporary Psychoanalys

Summary

1. Presentation i

2. The female subjectivity constitution:
A look by Freudian bias 11

3. The body image constitution 31

4. The Knives Man: A clinical study 45

5. Contemporary reflections on hysterical
and obsessive neurosis 61

6. French psychoanalyst Piera Aulagnier concept
about the neurosis psychopathology 77

7. The clinical method relevances for the
psychotherapy beginning 87

8. Psychoanalytic contributions of Karl
Abraham to the Freudian legacy 99

9. Doubt and guilty: A theoretical and clinical
study on the identificatory problem in an
obsessional neurosis case 109

10. The Rats Man case and his heritage for the
obsessional neurosis study 123

Presentation

In the comings and goings, the title The Walking Unconscious alludes to the plurality of the unconscious manifestations that this book attempts to comprise, from the female subjectivity conception to the contributions of contemporary psychoanalysts. The Unconscious needs to walk by the drives and the desire to achieve a joy that is not always sublime, but which alludes to the dosages of childish pleasures never before abandoned. It is this dose of pleasure that this reading aims to provide, through the lapse and associations that psychoanalysis provides to a reader who still, and unfortunately, is focused on the divan. Therefore, The Walking Unconscious is a point of arrival in which the subjectivity gains a new contour based on the Freudian work and his followers reading, such as Piera Aulagnier, Paul Schilder and Karl Abraham.

This book starts with a resumption of the femininity concept, which, starting from the penis envy concept, seeks to focus all the old infantile desire displacement within the femininity reach, as one of the possible exits of the Oedipus complex. And leaving this issue of the desire of desire or the non-desire, this refers to the work of Paul Schilder, emphasizing the body image formation, extolling how the pre-genital and infant genital phases are crucial for its understanding. The image of today is the result of an image already incorporated in the relationship between the mother and the baby; but as this is incorporated, and the way the pulsatory drives are formulated are decisive for this image constitution. So, this article seeks to resume its formation and possible distortions, highlighting the incorporation and projection mechanisms for its constitution.

Taking advantage of the Freudian theory context and metapsychology, this book also brings two studies of clinical cases:

the first titled as the Knives Man and the second as the clinical case of Paulo. But what is singular in these cases?

The Knives Man presented an unusual ritual: the knives, needles and other objects hiding in his house. What would be at the root of this ritual? What did this patient want to express in his symptoms? So, this study investigates the obsessional neurosis richness, a pathology that is resumed throughout this book by means of contemporary reflections, where the symptomatic positivity issue of this neurosis is highlighted, establishing a wide reflection based on the symptomatic relationship of this psychopathology, differentiating it from the obsessive compulsive disorder. On the pillars and roots of this neurosis, the doubt and guilt richness is explored in the clinical case of Paulo, distinguishing the relevance of the identificatory problem for understanding these two obsessional symptoms. So, based on the uniqueness of the clinical case of Paulo, the ambivalences and the identificatory building is pointed out for understanding its symptomatology

In the meanders of the reflections present in this book, by another optics, the book establishes a counterpoint with hysteria. Is this neurosis outdated? Or is it camouflaged in our current society? This is issue that many of these reflections are intended to respond, establishing a dialogue with the life drive so present in its etiology.

In this walking, where the unconscious creates symbolic feet and abstract bodies, this book also makes use of Karl Abraham and Piera Aulagnier contributions. If Abraham opened the doors to a new understanding of melancholy and psychosis, influencing the whole English school (primarily the Klenians), Aulagnier, in the French school, brings from Jacques Lacan a vision of psychopathology from the identificatory building. Thus, to understand the contributions of both, a resumption of their main postulates becomes the guiding axis for understanding many psychopathologies; but what is unique in each of these psychoanalysts, only a unique reading of this book can answer.

Therefore, through this multi-faceted plurality, this book seeks to break the old dilemma that psychoanalysis is an outdated science. In my understanding, it has never been so present in our context, but the blindness caused by the empirical search for instant results placed it in an area never before assigned, a space in which the anguish needs to be opened and the unconscious put into action: that is why the title of Walking Unconscious. The unconscious needs to walk through the other sciences: it has always been present, in latent state, but its own legs were never given. These symbolic legs are what allow a reflection that will lead the reader to a walking since the female subjectivity constitution to the obsessions clinic, passing by the hysteria, the body image and contemporary reflections. Let us read it!!!

The female subjectivity constitution: A look by Freudian bias

This chapter aims to address the female psychic subject constitution according to the Freudian theory. For this purpose, it is necessary to go through the Viennese master early studies on the psychic constitution.

At the end of the 19th century, the time corresponding to the start of psychoanalytic theory pillars, Freud is at the beginning of his study on the psychic subject constitution. When writing the letter number twenty-four to Fliess, Freud (1895) notes:

> After periods of ten to eleven hours with the neurosis [...] I am tormented by two objectives; examine what form the mental functioning theory will assume [...] and, secondly, extract from psychopathology a profit for the normal psychology. Actually, it is impossible to have a satisfactory general conception of neuropsychotic disorders if you cannot link it to clear assumptions about the normal mental processes.

So, in 1895, Freud is in the early days of the studies on the neurotic and normal processes. That same year, he focuses, on the text *Project for a Scientific Psychology*, the importance of another presence, usually the mother, at the beginning of the baby's life, for his psychic development.

According to Freud, in the psychic apparatus origin, the tension state present in the baby body, generated by the hungry tries to be released by means of a motor discharge, such as screaming and crying; but no motor discharge leads to a result of his internal tension relief. The newborn body is incapable of a specific action that extinguished the tension state, needing the help from another person. That is, of a foreign help, from his mother (or from a substitute) through a specific action. In this way, the satisfaction experience puts an end to the child internal tension through the mother (or substitute) external aid to her son, having this experience more radical implications in the development of an individual functions.

Freud resumes the experience importance in the psychic constitution satisfaction in Chapter VII of his book *The Dreams Interpretations.* In this famous book, Freud notes that the satisfaction experience introduces the baby desire, conceiving the desire as "a psychic notion which will seek there-cathexis of mnemonic image perception and revoke the own perception, which is to reestablish the original satisfaction situation." (1900, p. 595). He postulates that only desire is capable of putting the psychic apparatus in motion, in accordance with the pleasure principle. Thus, in the psychic constitution a first moment, when the internal tension state created by the need arises again, the satisfactory object image is reinvested as the desire hallucinatory satisfaction.

But when publishing the text *Formulations On Mental Functioning Two Principles*, Freud points out:

> It will be objected that an organization that was slave of the pleasure principle and disregarded the external world reality could not keep alive, even for a shorter time [...] The use of a fiction like this, however, is justified when one considers the baby – provided that he contains the care received from the mother – almost performing a psychic system of this kind (1911, p. 238).

Freud, in this quotation, is referring to the reality principle introduction in the baby psychic constitution first moments. So, after the satisfaction experience, as there is an increasing requirement of internal needs and, consequently an absence of expected satisfaction, the child abandons this satisfaction attempt through the hallucination. And due to the lack of satisfaction through the hallucination, a new principle of mental functioning is started: the reality principle.

After the first satisfaction experience the child desired is established, the Viennese master stresses the newborn maternal cares importance. In 1905, in the *Three Essays on Sexuality Theory,* he reiterates the importance assigned to the other, who usually is the maternal figure, in the child sexuality establishment. Thus, Freud states that:

> The child deals with the person who assists him, for him, a constant source of excitement and sexual satisfaction from erogenous zones, and even more if this person, usually the mother, admires the child with the feelings derived from her own sexual life: she touches, kisses and cradles, and it is perfectly clear that she treats him as the replacement of a fully legitimate sexual object [...] She [the mother] is awakening the her son sexual drive and preparing its later intensity (1905, p. 210-211).

The mother (or someone who replaces her), when taking care of the baby caressing and kissing him, is awakening his sexual drive or libido. The mother (or someone who represents her) offers an endless source of sexual excitement and satisfaction of erogenous zones for her child.

And when referring to the life and death drive presence at the child early psychic constitution, Freud (1923) postulates that life emergence would be, then, the life continuation and also, at the same time, the effort towards death. And life itself would be a conflict and a reconciliation of these two inclinations. These two inclinations are two drive classes that coexist since birth: the life drive (sexual drive or libido and self-preservation drive) and the death drive (destructive drive, domain or power will). Life consists of conflict manifestations or the interaction between these two impulsive classes, i.e., between life drive (Eros) and death drive (Thanatos).

These two drive classes are present in human psyche, but Freud notes that, at the beginning, "the libido has the mission to make the destructor instinct innocuous and performs it diverting this instinct, mainly, outside [...] with the aid of a special organic system, the muscular apparatus" (1924, p. 181). The death drive deviation to the external environment is essential for the psyche constitution. The life drive aims to make the destructive and aggressive drive harmless, partially directing it to outside and, partially, by mixing with it.

During the first maternal cares that the individual sexual drive arises, Freud points out:

> The child lips behave as an erogenous zone, and the stimulation by the warm milk was, no doubt, the source of pleasurable sensation [...]. Sexual activity primarily relies on one of the functions that serve for the life preservation, and only later becomes independent from them (1905, p. 171).

Early in life, the baby's sexual pleasure comes from the moth-lips excitement, the tongue. At this time, sexual activity can be related to milk intake, the lips stimulation etc.

In addition to providing that sexual pleasure, the affectionate relationship between baby and mother becomes a model for all loving relationships in the individual life. Freud (1905) declares that the object encounter [at puberty] is, in fact, a re-encounter. This means that even after the sexual activity is separated from the nutrition act, a significant portion remains to prepare the boy and girl to the puberty object choice, being this object encounter a re-encounter of the old love object abandoned in remote childhood, after the Oedipus complex resolution.

From birth, the Viennese master underlines the parents' presence importance (and not only the mother) on the son psychic constitution. In relation to this presence, Freud explains:

> So they [the parents] are under the compulsion of assigning all perfections to the son [...] and hiding and forgetting all his deficiencies [...] He will once again really be the center and the creation essence – 'His Majesty the Baby' [...] The child will materialize his golden dreams that parents have never realized [...] The parents love, so touching and in fact so childish, is nothing more than the parents narcissism reborn, which, transformed into love object, unmistakably revels its previous nature (1914, p. 97).

For Freud, concomitantly to the mother presence, the father is also present since the child early psychic constitution. The child birth represents for the couple (here understood as father and mother) a revival of their own narcissism that had been long abandoned. So, mom and dad relieve the old childish narcissism with their child birth, assigning all the world perfections to this new son, and denying his faults and imperfections.

According to the Freudian metapsychology, in addition to the parents' old narcissism revival with the son birth, the self-eroticism and the narcissism deserve a brief highlight in the male subject psychic constitution.

In a letter to Fliess, Freud (1899) already defined the self-eroticism as a lower sexual layer [...] that acts without any psychosexual objective and only requires the local sensations of satisfaction.

Six years after writing this letter, Freud writes the *Three Essays*. In this brilliant book, which caused (and still causes) criticism to psychoanalysis, Freud (1905) expresses that, in early life, the drive was not directed to another person; it is satisfied in the own body, it is the self-erotic. That is, the baby presents the mode by which sexual drive finds satisfaction in his own body. And this mode is referred to as self-eroticism.

It is necessary to point out that, for Freud (1914):

A unit comparable to ego cannot exist in the individual since the beginning; ego has to be developed. The
self-erotic drives, however, have been there since the beginning, and therefore, it is necessary that something is
added to the self-eroticism – a new psychic action – in
order to provoke the narcissism (1914, p. 84).

Thus, the self-eroticism, i.e. the mode by which the drive
seeks satisfaction in the subject own body, is present since the
beginning. Narcissism is the result of a new psychic action which
would be added to self-eroticism.

Although not specified in the text *Regarding Narcissism:
an introduction* (1914) what is this psychic action, in the article
The Drives and its Vicissitudes, Freud (1915) says:

We are used to denote the ego development initial
phase, during which the sexual instincts find self-erotic
satisfaction, of 'narcissism' [...]. At the very beginning
of life, ego is the cathexis with the instincts, being, to a
certain extent, able to satisfy them in ourselves. We call
this 'narcissism' condition, and this form of obtaining
satisfaction, 'self-erotic'. (1915, p. 137-139).

In this text, he understands narcissism as a first way in
which ego is constituted, because thanks to 'his majesty, the
baby'; the child's ego is organized in its early form as an ideal
ego, narcissistically invested by libido and which masterpiece the
boy is not willing to renounce during his childhood. Thus, the
ego is a unit that does not exist since the psychic constitution
beginning, needing to become, as an ideal ego, narcissistically
invested by the parents.

It seems necessary to point out that for Freud, before the
ideal ego resulting in narcissism, the ego is "first and foremost, a
body ego; and not simply a surface entity, but it is [...] the projection of a surface" (1923, p. 42). In the psychic early constitution,

the newborn is provided of an id and, then, a body ego, targeting to the establishment of an ideal ego narcissistically invested.

On the subject psychic constitution, in addition to the ideal ego presence, it is necessary to point out the role played by pre-genital organizations.

In libidinal development level, Freud (1904) postulates that during the early years of a child's life there are organizations in which the genital areas have not assumed its predominant role. These organizations are defined as pre-genital organizations in which the drives are partial and which objective is the satisfaction by means of appropriate stimulation of erogenous zone.

Freud (1905) defines erogenous zone as a part of the skin or the mucosa where certain types of stimulation cause pleasurable feeling of certain quality. These dominant areas are, respectively, the mouth in the oral phase and the anus in the anal phase. Still, according to Freud (1905), the first of these pre-genital sexual organizations is the oral, or [...] cannibalistic. In this, the sexual activity has not yet separated from nutrition, or the differentiated opposing currents inside it.

In this organization, sexual activity is related to the nutrition and which erogenous dominant zone is the mouth. During this organization, the child feels pleasure sucking the mother breast. That is, at the beginning of the baby's life, the psychic activity focuses on providing satisfaction to oral zones needs, such as sucking the milk from the mother breast and subsequently sucking (somehow) another object that replaces the breast, such as the finger or pacifier. The act of sucking on the mother breast is the first activity that provides pleasure to the baby, where his lips behave as an erogenous zone. Thus, sexuality begins to manifest in the baby and after breastfeeding, when he starts sucking the breast, finger or pacifier.

During the oral organization, Freud (1905), declares that the sexual target consists in the incorporation of the object, model that later will play, in the form of identification, a psychic important role.

For Freud, the second pre-genital organization is the anal-sadist which dominant erogenous zone is the anal. In this organization, Freud says:

> The intestinal contents [...] have for the breastfeeding other important senses. It is obviously treated as a part of his own body, representing the first 'gift'. When disposing of it, the little creature can express docility to the environment surrounding him, and when refusing it, his stubbornness (1905, p. 176).

During the anal-sadistic organization, the faeces represent the first gift that the child can give someone that he likes, demonstrating his obedience. If he denies giving the faeces, he is expressing his stubbornness.

Freud explains that "the fecal mass retention, at first intentionally practiced to take advantage of the stimulation as an anal zone masturbatory [...] and, incidentally, one of the causes of constipation so frequent in neuropaths." (1905, p. 176). The fecal mass retention during childhood may be related to masturbatory stimulation of anal zone, as he can also be demonstrating his pertinacity in the relationship with the people who take care of this child. And when growing, this game of retaining faeces may be symbolically present in the special scatological rituals, in ceremonial acts and similar acts which are carefully kept confidential by the neurotic individual.

Freud (1913) points out that in anal-sadistic organization the genital zones primacy has not yet been established. On the contrary, the instinct components that dominate this pre-genital organization of sexual life or the anal-erotic and sadistic.

In a note added to *Three Essays*, Freud (1905) recognizes that in this organization the division into opposites that pervades the sexual life is already constituted, but they still cannot be called masculine and feminine, but active and passive.

During this pre-genital organization, the active inclination is filled by the domain instinct that Freud calls sadism and the passive inclination is fueled by the anal eroticism. A fortification of anal eroticism allows an inclination to homosexuality in males when the genitals primacy is achieved.

On the *New Conferences*, Freud notes that:

> The attitude towards the libido organization phases has changed a bit [...]. Whereas, previously, it mainly emphasized the way how each phase passed before the next phase, our attention, now, is directed to the facts that show how much of each prior phase still continues in the subsequent configurations [...] (1933, p. 102).

Namely, the predominance of one phase in relation to the other does not occur so suddenly, but gradually, since parts of the previous organization always coexist side by side the latest.

In another footnote added to *Three Essays*, Freud (1905) revels that "after the two pre-genital organizations, there is a third phase in child development: this, that already deserves the name of genital [...] knows only one type of genitalia: the male. For this reason I called it the organization phallic phase" (1905, p. 188). The third organization described by Freud is the infant genital organization, in which, to the phallus primacy, is also called phallic phase. In this phase culminate the Oedipus complex and the castration complex.

For the Viennese master:

> The main characteristic of this "infant genital organization" is its difference from the adult final genital organization. It consists in the fact that, for both sexes, only one genital organ is considered, namely, the male. What is present, therefore, is not a priority of the genitals, but the phallus primacy. (1923, p. 158).

At this phase, both the boys and the girls only recognize one genital organ: the male. The observation of this organ is of utmost relevance, since the losing fantasy traces different destinations in both sexes: if, for the girl, the castration anxiety that launches her on the Oedipus complex, for the boy, it is the same anxiety that 'demolishes' this complex. For a better understanding of how this complex, articulated to the castration complex, occurs in the female, we would like to turn to the Oedipus complex in females.

Female Oedipus Complex

In the text *The Infant Genital Organization* Freud no longer addresses the idea of symmetry between the male and female Oedipus complex, and points out that the phallus primacy, in the phallic phase, is of extreme relevance to the individual psychic destiny. In my understanding, the castration will focus on this primacy (both in the boy and girl) breaking the false narcissistic illusion of being the response to maternal desire. And when finishing this article, he points out that he "can only describe this state of things at the point at which it affects male child; the processes [...] in the girl we do not know" (1923, p. 180). Thus, the female Oedipus complex was still unknown at this time and, over the subsequent years; he devoted special attention to it.

In 1924, the master states that "the girl Oedipus complex in girls is much simpler than the penis small carrier" (1924, p. 119). At this time, the girl desires to assume the space occupied by her mother, assuming a female attitude in relation to the father. Not satisfied with this observation, and rethinking the articulations game of positive and negative sides in this complex, Freud, in 1925, points out the castration anxiety importance.

Such observation occurs in the article *Some Psychic Conse-*

quences of Anatomical Distinction Between the Sexes in which he brings an articulation between the Oedipus complex and castration complex (and, consequently, with the phallic phase). In the case of the girl, the castration complex inserts her on the Oedipus complex, taking her from a negative side in relation to the mother and playing in a positive relation regarding the father. In these intricacies, castration anxiety is settled in the girl due to the fact of missing this organ: in her fantasies, the penis was withdrawn, leaving her out of this organ. About this, Mijolla understands that "girls are castrated boys as a punishment for her incestuous desires and masturbation" (2005, p.373).

Due to the fact of being deprived of this organ by her mother, the girl seeks reparation with the father. Thus, when discovering her organic inferiority, it is with much hesitation and reluctance that the girl accepts this unpleasant knowledge and imagines that one day she will be able to have this organ. Consequently, this leaves a negative relation with the mother, displacing to a positive Oedipal relationship with the father.

In these disconnection mishaps, the master introduces the penis envy issue to girls, as well as the desire to have children. This means that, when she discovers she is deprived of this organ, the girl disconnects from the mother and seeks the different sex (the father), expressing the desire to have a son with him, while in the past she wished to have one from her mother. Thus, the Oedipal complex entire development is concrete in the penile envy shadow.

Here it is interesting to note that the mother is a common and first element at the male and female Oedipus complex beginning. Both the boy and the girl should renounce this object, once the castration anguish makes both see as castrated, collapsing the maternal phallus. If, on the other hand, the girl comes to refuse such a perception, such fact could generate the psychosis; but, if on the other hand, she accepts it, she can be taken by the penis envy, since her mother deprived her from this organ, and the only one who could provide it would be her father. So, against this envy, the girl turns away resentful of the mother for the damage caused and in search of her father for the desire of having a penis and, subsequently, the desire to have a son with him, becoming "a little woman" (1925, p. 318).

According to Freud, the positive Oedipus complex in women "can be slowly abandoned or dealt with repression, and its effects can persist with a lot of emphasis on women mental life" (1925, p. 319). At this point, I believe that the master already alludes, indirectly, to the fear of maternal love loss as a primary factor in the female Oedipus complex resolution.

Six years were not enough for Freud examining this complex specificity deeper. In his article *Female Sexuality*, he highlights that the recognition of female castration opens three psychic possible destinations.

The first possible way would be the general revulsion to sexuality. This means that the girl scarred by the comparison with the boys, grows dissatisfied with her clitoris, abandoning her phallic activity and, with it, her general sexuality. This girl lived in a male way: she could get pleasure from her clitoris, keeping this activity in relation to her wishes directed to the mother. Thus, her homoerotic love was directed to the phallic mother and when she discovers this is castrated, it becomes possible to abandon her as an object, creating a hostility relationship.

The second path, through the castration anguish, would be the masculinity complex. This makes the girl to adopt a challenging measure regarding her threatened masculinity, holding on the hopes of getting a penis in any occasion. She refuses to recognize the fact observed and, in a defiant manner, becomes involved with her clitoral activity and refuges in an identification with her phallic mother of with her father. It would be in this hope that the fantasy of being a man persists, resulting, from this complex, the choice of her manifest homosexual object. Therefore, if a girl persists in the desire to turn into a boy, she will end up a manifest homosexual, or, in some cases, she may present traits for men through her adult genital organization.

If the Oedipus complex development follows a third path, the girl will achieve a normal female normal attitude, making the father as the desire object and thus finding a path to the Oedipus complex feminine form. At this time, the girl leaves the mother she loved, since she cannot forgive her for having her deprived of a penis, and puts the father as her love object. And when losing the old love object, the girl identifies with her, occupying the place of this ancient connection. This means that, when putting on the mother place, she tries to take her place with the father, being the hatred a result of this link. This hatred comes from the penis envy and mortification which was denied to her.

So, the girl goes towards the father wishing to have a penis that she was deprived, although such desire leads to another desire: of having a baby from him as a gift. At this moment, the desire to have a baby will occupy the former desire to have a penis.

For Freud, in women, "the Oedipus complex constitutes the final result of a quite lengthy development. This is not destroyed, but created by the castration influence" (1931, p. 238). The rivalry attitude with her mother originates before from the female Oedipal complex, being strengthened and exploited in the Oedipal situation.

This distance from the mother is "a very important step in the course of a girl development" (1931, p.247). The girl in the positive Oedipus complex leads to a change in the loving object (from the mother to the father), as well as a change in the erogenous zone (from the clitoris to the vagina). As in psychoanalysis there is no overcoming of a previous phase to the next one, in the case of women, the oral, anal, clitoral, vaginal, and body eroticism are present in sexual pleasure, and it is not correct to say that the clitoral pleasure should be overcome by the vaginal.

The pleasure obtained by the pleasurable sensations of

clitoral handling is reintegrated in the article titled *Femininity*, when the master says: "the little girls do the same with her small clitoris. It seems that, in all of the, the masturbatory activity is performed in this equivalent to the penis, and that the truly feminine vagina, at this time, has not been discovered yet by both sexes" (1933, p. 118). In the phallic phase, the clitoris is the primary erogenous zone and, if the girl goes towards femininity, this pleasure is displaced to the vagina.

So, during the infant genital organization, the girl needs to change her erogenous zone (from clitoris to vagina) and object (from mother to father), although the pre-Oedipal link with the mother is of extreme relevance to the understanding of adulthood conflicts. Consequently, the distance from the mother can end in hatred, since this object change comes with hostility, since this mother deprived the organ that she desires.

According to Freud, the girl can only progress to assume her femininity if this desires to obtain the father penis is replaced by the desire to have a baby, making this baby a symbolic equivalent to the old penis that one day she wished to obtain. Therefore, with the transfer to the father of the penis-baby desire, the girl starts the Oedipus complex situation, fortifying the hostility against her mother, since this rival received from the father what the girl one day wanted to have. That is why reaching femininity supposes three phases.

The first phase proposes that the castration recognition leads the girl to resent her mother for not giving her a penis, going away from her with hostility, although she keeps the love-hate ambivalence with her. In the second phase, she is taken by the penis envy, searching for the father. In the third and final phase, this girl turns to her father in order to win a penis that the mother refused. Consequently, the female situation will come true if the desire to have the penis is replace by the desire to have a baby, making this baby to assume the penis place.

According to Freud, in the girl, "the Oedipal situation is the result of a long and hard evolution; it is a kind of preliminary solution, a rest position that is not soon abandoned, especially because the latency period beginning is not so far" (1933, p. 128). So, the girls remain in the Oedipus complex for an indeterminate time, they destroy it belatedly and, yet, "incomplete" (1933, p. 129). Due to this, the superego does not reach intensity, such as it occurs with the boys.

In *Anxiety and Instinctive Life*, Freud takes up this demolition, stating:

> The castration fear is not, of course, the only reason for repression: in fact, it does not happen with women, because, although they have a castration complex, they cannot have fear of being castrated. In her sex, what happens is the fear of maternal love loss, which is, evidently, a later extension of the child's anxiety when noticing the mother absence (1933, p. 90).

Therefore, to the psychoanalysis father, what leads a girl to an end to her Oedipus complex, establishing the superego is the fear of maternal love loss.

However, I would like to point out that humans sex life has a apex from three to five years of age, declining around this age, being followed, first, by a latency period and, subsequently, by the adult genital organization.

During this organization, Freud declares that "little loss is caused to a woman if she stays in her feminine Oedipal attitude" (1940, p. 207). Thus, in her adulthood, she may choose the husband by her paternal characteristics, recognizing his authority. The old desire to possess a penis is supported if she is successful in the choice of this loving object, extending her love to the organ carrier.

Ego Ideal and the superego.

When referring to the ego ideal formation, Freud (1914) states:

> For the ego, the formation of an ideal would be a conditioning factor of repression [...]. What the subject projects towards himself as being his ideal [of ego] is the replacement for narcissism lost in his childhood in which his own ideal was [...]. The ego development consists in the removal of his primary narcissism [...]. This distance is caused by the libido displacement towards an externally imposed ego ideal (1914, p. 100-102).

Thus, during the pre-genital and infant genital organization there is a narcissistic invested ideal ego. Due to the castration anxiety during the phallic phase, there is the infantile sexuality and ideal ego repression, which heirs are, as stated in the previous paragraph, the superego and the ideal ego. This ideal ego is the narcissism replacement lost in childhood.

When writing *The Ego and the Id*, Freud (1923) stresses that the differentiation with the ego can be called 'ego ideal' or 'superego'. At this time, Freud uses both concepts interchangeably, but it is only in the *New Conferences* that he elaborates a differentiation between superego and ideal ego. In these conferences, Freud (1933[1932]) declares that superego is:

> The ego ideal vehicle, by which the ego is evaluated, that stimulates it and which requirements for perfection are always greater than what he strives to accomplish [...]. This ego ideal is the precipitate of the parents old image, the admiration expression that the child so attributed to them (1933, p. 70).

I understand that Freud imputes to the superego a function of being the ego ideal vehicle responsible for the perfection pursuit, and the superego for the ego ideal maintenance. Its functions are the self-observation, the consciousness and the maintenance of this ideal. On the other hand, the ego ideal has the function to stimulate the ego to achieve perfection and serve as an instrument through which ego evaluates itself.

On superego formation, Freud (1924) considers that the father or both parents authority is introjected in ego, and there forms the superego core, which assumes the father severity and perpetuates this prohibition against incest, thus defeating the ego of libidinal cathexis return. Superego retains the strength, severity, and the inclination to punish that is inherited from parents. This psychic instance protects the ego against the incestuous desires return.

For Freud:

> The child superego is, in fact, built not according to the his parents model, but his parents superego [...] It becomes a tradition vehicle and all of long lasting value judgments that this way were transmitted from generation to generation (1933, p. 69).

Then, the superego of a boy is above all, a psychic instance when the values that go beyond his parents' superego are present, since the values and judgments are transmitted from generation to generation.

After the latency phase (where we found the superego formation according to the Freudian conception), there begins the adult genital organization. In this organization, the "[Oedipus] complex is unconsciously revived and involved in new modifications" (1924, p. 263). At puberty, man revives in his unconscious the old Oedipal complex repressed in his early childhood. In this organization, the sexual drives are in the reproduction service. During puberty that one can establish a clear separation between the male and female characters, establishing the genital areas macy that was not possible in the child genital organization. At this phase, the woman can present an object choice of analytical or connection object type, since during her puberty when the adult sexual life final configuration occurs, when the object encounter is consummated, which had been prepared from the most remote childhood.

Conclusion

Throughout this article the core concepts linked to psychic constitution of female subject in Freudian theory were crossed, but it is necessary to highlight that due to the Oedipal complex articulation with the castration complex, each subject may present three possible exits for his infantile sexuality, i.e., three psychic destinations: neurosis, psychosis and perversion. While that, for Freud (1924), in neurosis there is the castration recognition, in psychosis occurs the refusal of this, being the delirium a bridge to the reality exclusion. And in perversion there is a recognition, and the castration refusal, being the fetishism its prototype.

Therefore, before making a diagnosis of each clinical case, the psychotherapist is entitled to recognize his patient in the symptom singularity, listening to his libidinal and identificatory story. It is from his listening that the concepts listed above will create liveliness in the clinical practice, allowing the construction of a clinical listening.

Bibliographical Reference

FREUD, S. (1950/1996). *Project for a Scientific Psychology. ESB, vol. I, Rio de Janeiro:* Imago.

_____. (1900/1996). *The Dreams Interpretation. ESB, vol. V, Rio de Janeiro:* Imago.

_____. (1905/1996). *Three Essays On the Sexuality Theory. ESB,* vol. VII, Rio de Janeiro: Imago.

_____. (1908/1996). *Character and Anal Eroticism. ESB, vol. IX, Rio de Janeiro:* Imago.

_____. (1908/1996). *On the Sexual Theories of Children. ESB,* vol. IX, Rio de Janeiro: Imago.

_____. (1911/1996). *Formulations On the Two Principles of Mental Functioning. ESB,* vol. XII, Rio de Janeiro: Imago.

_____. (1912/1996). *Contributions to a Debate on Masturbation. ESB,* vol. XII, Rio de Janeiro: Imago.

_____. (1914/1996). *On the Narcissism: An Introduction. ESB,* vol. XIV, Rio de Janeiro: Imago.

_____. (1915/1996). *The Instincts and its Vicissitudes. ESB,* vol. XIV, Rio de Janeiro: Imago.

_____. (1915/1996). *Repression.ESB,* vol. XIV, Rio de Janeiro: Imago.

_____. (1917/1996). *Conference XIX – Resistance and Repression. ESB,* vol. XVI, Rio de Janeiro: Imago.

_____. (1920/1996). *Group Psychology and the Ego Analysis. ESB,* vol. XVIII, Rio de Janeiro: Imago.

_____. (1923/1996). *The Ego and the Id ESB,* vol. XIX, Rio de Janeiro: Imago.

_____. (1923/1996). *The Infant Genital Organization: An Interpolation of Sexuality Theory. ESB,* vol. XIX, Rio de Janeiro: Imago.

_____. (1924/1996). *The Masochism Economic Problem. ESB,* vol. XIX, Rio de Janeiro: Imago.

_____. (1924/1996). *The Dissolution of the Oedipus Complex.* *ESB*, vol. XIX, Rio de Janeiro: Imago.

_____. (1924/1996). *Neurosis and Psychosis.* *ESB*, vol. XIX, Rio de Janeiro: Imago.

_____. (1925/1996). *Some Psychic Consequences of Anatomical Distinction Between the Sexes.* *ESB*, vol. XIX, Rio de Janeiro: Imago.

_____. (1926/1996). *Inhibitions, Symptoms and Anxiety.* *ESB*, vol. XX, Rio de Janeiro: Imago.

_____ (1931/1996). *Female Sexuality.* *ESB*, vol. XXI, Rio de Janeiro: Imago.

_____. (1933/1996). *Conference XXXI – The Psychic Personality Dissection.ESB*, vol. XXII, Rio de Janeiro: Imago.

_____. (1933/1996). *Conference XXXII – Anxiety and Instinctive Life.ESB*, vol. XXII, Rio de Janeiro: Imago.

_____. (1933/1996). *Conference XXXIII - Femininity.* *ESB*, vol. XXII, Rio de Janeiro: Imago.

_____. (1940/1996). *Psychoanalysis Outline.* *ESB*, vol. XXIII, Rio de Janeiro: Imago.

MASSON, J. M. (1986). *The complete correspondence of Sigmund Freud to Wilhelm Fliess 1887-1904.*Rio de Janeiro: Imago.

The body image constitution

Introduction

This article seeks to focus on the neurologist Paul Schilder vision on the body image formation, based on a literature review of his work entitled *The Body Image: the psyche constructive energies*. For starting this discussion, how does Schilder understand body image?

According to Schilder (1935, p. 11) "body image is understood as the figuration of our body formed in our minds; i.e., the way the body is presented to us".

The body schema (also understood as body image) is the three-dimensional image that all people have of themselves. In this three-dimensional aspect we have the psychological, sociological and physiological aspects.

For Schilder (1935, p. 15), "when studding the body image, we should address the central psychological problem of the relation between the impressions of our senses, our movements, and the general motility". This means that the body schema is in perpetual self-construction, living in continuous differentiation and integration. On the other hand, our body postural model relates to the postural model of other bodies. Our body image experience and other bodies experience are closely interconnected. Therefore, the emotions, actions and perceptions are inseparable from our body image. They contribute to our body image construction.

Material and method

The method to be used in this article is supported in a bibliographical survey on the work entitled *The Body Image: The Psyche Constructive Energies*, published in 1935, which seeks to give prominence to the sociological and psychological aspects of body image constitution, emphasizing the erogenous zones, the libidinal phases and the social aspects throughout its constitution.

Results

First, to Schilder (1935), the body image begins to form from birth. Namely, since birth, two factors have special participation in the body image creation: one is the pain and the other is the members' motor control.

The pain helps us decide what we want to get closer to the ego and what we want to maintain the furthest possible from it. In addition, the visual experience has a leading role in the body image formation. This experience is also lived through the action. In other words, it is through the actions and determinations that we give the final shape to our body ego. Thus, the visual impressions influence the body schema, since body image can be disturbed by experimental changes in vision, but it is restructured, forming a new unit.

For Schilder (1935, p. 60) "the body schema development also occurs parallel to the motor sensory development". Throughout the psychic development, the movement leads to a better guidance in relation to our body. We do not know much about the body, unless we move it. The movement is an important factor of unification of our body different parts and through it we come to a definite relationship with the outside world and with the objects, and only through the contact with the outside that we become able to correlate the various impressions about our body. The knowledge of our body depends, in large part, of our own action. Thus, since birth, the body postural model needs to be built. It is a creation and a construction, the production of a shape. The structuring process is only possible when it closely relates with the world experiences.

For Schilder (1935, p. 102) "the body image, in its final result, is a unit. But this unit is not rigid, but liable of transformation. And all the senses are always contributions to the body scheme creation". In other words, the visual perceptions strongly influence the body image. The images change under the drives and motor imagination influences. Schilder (1935) argues that these distortions are called metamorphosias. Among these, we have polyopia that would be the tendency to multiply the visual image, becoming larger (macropsia) or smaller (micropsia)

The Libidinal Structure of Body Image

Schilder uses the psychoanalytic theory to explain the libidinal structure of body image.

In his understanding of the psychoanalytic work, Schilder (1935, p. 107) points out that "we are interested in our body integrity". He claims that the libido belongs to our own body. He declares that, in principle, libido is given to the body as a whole. This is the narcissistic stage. In this phase, the child only cares for herself. This stage, referred to as primary narcissism, is followed by an autoerotic phase, in which the libido is focused on body parts that have special erogenous signification. Concomitantly to auto-eroticism, Schilder describes the pre-genital and child genital phases.

The first phase or would be oral phase. In this, the milk intake occurs and the erogenous zone is the mouth. At this phase, the body tries to incorporate the outside world, which is only considered according to its ability to produce (or not) satisfaction. At this point, the child also enjoys the sensations from the skin. There is a cutaneous eroticism.

In the oral phase, aggression can also occur aiming to destroy the mother breast. This aggressiveness (and consequently, the sadism) can persist in the anal phase.

The second phase is the anal-sadistic phase. In this there is pleasure in defecation and the erogenous zone is the anus. During this phase, the outside world receives an interest portion from the child, occurring anal and homosexual tendencies in relation to external objects.

The third phase would be the phallic, which coincides with the Oedipus Complex (nuclear complex of the psychic subject constitution). At this phase, the genitals acquire a new meaning and become the main libidinal zone in the body. At this phase there is a complete understanding of the child's body as something opposite to the outside world. After the end of the Oedipus complex, we have the secondary narcissism aspect, a moment when the libido is withdrawn from "outside world".

According to Schilder reading, narcissism is seen as a large (libidinal) reservoir which lends part of its contents to the objects. The energy that was withdrawn from this reservoir can be brought back at any time. And what is the relationship between the primary narcissism and the body image? For Schilder (1935), any libido or energy of ego desires can only appear in connection with an object. We are in a world, and the objects are part of it. When we live, we are facing this world. There is always a person and this person attitude. An attitude is an attitude to something: the narcissistic libido object is the body image. But there is no doubt that our body can only exist as part of the world.

For the newborn, body and world are interconnected experiences. One is not possible without the other. In so primitive level, the boundary between body and world is not clearly defined. It will be easier to perceive a part of the body in the world than a part of the world in the body. Thus, the body will be projected in the world, and this will be introjected in the body. And in adulthood, body and world are in constant exchange.

Thus, at birth there is a zone of lack of differentiation between body and world. But the body image has to be developed and built. Libido is linked to the different parts of body image and, in various phases of libido development, the body model will continuously change.

In the body scheme overall structure, the erogenous zones will have a leading role. In other words, we can assume that the body image, during the oral phase of development, will be centered in the mouth and, in anal phase, in the anus. The libidinal flow of energy will greatly influence the body image. And during the body image construction, there will be a continuous interaction between ego and id.

Erogenous Zones of Body Image

For Schilder (1935, p. 142) "the own organs [of the body] force the individual to a continuous contact with the outside world, and there is no doubt that, at least in part, we discover our body through these contacts". The enormous psychological importance of every orifice of the body is present since birth. Through the mouth we eat the food. Andin adulthood, by means of certain cavities we eject urine, sexual products, faeces and air. In addition, the body surface is also an erogenous zone. The skin is easily irritable and, consequently, it is an irritation organ. There are continuous sensations that lead the child to touch or make people around him touch his skin.

It is very important to note that much of the body is discovered by the hands. In addition to the hand and look, the contact with the others (fathers, mothers, friends and neighbors) and the interest that these demonstrate to the various parts of our body will be of huge importance for the development of the body postural model; since "whenever a part of our body image receives excessive importance, the symmetry and the internal balance of body image are destroyed" (Schilder, 1935, p. 113). Therefore, the organic pain (that leads the body model libidinal structure to change immediately), the organic diseases, the erogenous zones, our hands action on the body, the others actions regarding our body, the others interest by our body are important factors for the body image final structuring.

In addition, the libidinal structures differences reflect in the body postural model structure. Individuals in whom a partial desire is increased will feel a certain point of the body, the particular erogenous zone belonging to the desire, in the center of his body images, as if the energy was accumulated in certain points. There are energy lines connecting different erogenous zones and we will have variations in the body image structuring, according to the individual psychosexual tendencies.

For Schilder (1935, p. 159) "every erogenous zone has typical extension lines". In adulthood there is the extension of these erogenous zones to certain parts of the body. The anal zone extends to the back. The mouth, usually, extends to the interior plan. In other words, extends to the hands, mouth and nose inner part. Therefore, it is impossible to study the libidinal structure of body image in isolation. It is an integral part of the individual internal vital history and, to understand it, it is necessary to study the libidinal development since childhood. Thus, our body knowledge is developed based on the continuously renewed contact with the outside world since childhood, and the body image construction is based not only on the person individual story, but also in his relations with others.

For Schilder (1935, p. 164) "the body schema is a unit that not only incorporates parts of the outside world, but also waives these. There is not only a tendency to structure the body postural model, but also to destroy this image". For example, when we eat food or drink, something from outside world is added to body image. After digestion, the intestinal movement just physically separates faeces from body, but psychologically, these continue to be part of us.

The anatomical configuration (of genital organs) plays an important role in body structure. A protuberance belongs less to the body; because whenever a body part connects less closely with the rest, there is a fear of losing it. It is the fear for body integrity, which is based on the postural model internal qualities.

In addition, the body postural model only remains stable for a short time, immediately changing. Probably, the psychic life figurations instability only connotes a passing phase with which the next phase can be contrasted. But there is no doubt that, in our psychic life, there are always tendencies to form units. But whenever a unit, a Gestalt is created, this immediately tends to change and destroy. Destruction is a partial phase of construction, which is a project and life general characteristic. Destroy to rebuild a new image.

Discussion

Libidinal Development of Body Image

Schilder, in his reading of Freudian work, points out that since the beginning of life there a nucleus of body image in the oral zone. Using Berfeld, Schilder (1935) admits that there is a primary development that begins in the oral zone and a secondary refinement that differentiates the body ego from the outside world. So, he points out:

"We have reasons to believe that there is an internal development, a maturation in all fields of psychic life, and that there are internal factors in the organism relatively independent of the experiences that determine this evolution. The maturation process acquires its final form from the individual experiences, which will depend, largely, on the vital experience, training and emotional activities" (SCHILDER, 1935, p. 179).

Our body image is not always the same. The body image evolution is, somewhat, parallel to the perceptions, thoughts and object relations development.

Every desire and every libidinal trend change immediately the body image structure. In any attitude, we desire to modify the postural model or body scheme spatial relationship. The minute we see something, muscular actions start leading to changes in its perception. All drive or desire modifies the body image, its gravity and its mass. Thus, in every action and every desire we intend to obtain a body image change.

For Schilder "the body image can shrink or expand, can give its parts to outside world or seize upon parts of it" (1935, p. 176). For example, the lips and face painting, hair discoloration and tattoo are attempts to change the body image. The meaning of all these changes of appearance is not always conscious; because there is a symbolic meaning, as for example, the skin cleaning can be considered an example of drive to overcome unconscious anal tendencies.

In addition to hygiene, clothes became a part of body image. That is, any piece of clothes dressed becomes, immediately, part of the body image.

As the clothes are part of the body schema, these gain the same sense of body parts and can represent various symbolic meanings. Consequently, all transformations found in body image can be found in the clothes. This means that clothes can become a means to entirely change our body image; and when imitating a famous person's clothes, we modify our postural image, incorporating others image. Therefore, the body images are not isolated entities. The body images community is the basis of all social function.

It is necessary to emphasize that body image passes through a continuous process of expansion and reduction. The primitive peoples and certain psychotic patients can modify body image through a simple process of libidinal imagination; for example, they transform an individual into a werewolf on the basis of their beliefs. People already considered 'neurotic' only achieve minor "autoplastic" modifications through masks and clothes.

Humans are surrounded and curtailed by their body images. One of the reasons for the transformation and use of clothes is the desire to overcome the rigidity of body image, which can be transformed through paintings, jewelry and etc.

The body can also be modified as a whole. We can make holes in the body or insert metal or wood pieces in it, as it occurred with the primitive peoples.

According to Schilder "one can also try to modify the body image in a less violent way, through all kinds of gymnastics" (1935, p. 179). So, the dance and gymnastics are ways to decrease the body postural model rigid shape. The dance leads to a disruption and a change of body image, leading us from a body image change to a psychic attitude change.

For Schilder (1935), we expand and contract the body postural model, we remove and add parts, we rebuild it; we mix details; create new details; we do this with our body and with its own expression. There is a construction and a destruction linked to the needs, conflicts and energy of the total personality. During the construction and destruction phases appear two basic human tendencies. One is the tendency to crystallize unities and ensure rest points, immutability and absence of change. The other is the tendency to obtain a continuous flow, a permanent change.

Beauty and Body Image

For Schilder "a beauty should be related to body postural model. When we consider the human figure beauty, we immediately realize that the aesthetic interest certainly relates closely with the interest in sex" (1935, p. 128). The human being beauty does not cause the desires immediately, but it brings inside the seeds of desires development, since the human figure beauty has a direct relation with sexuality.

Beauty is a social phenomenon. The human body, its postural model, is the first object of plastic arts and painting. The beauty object causes sexual drives without satisfying them; but, at the same time, allows everyone to enjoy it. The beauty is, also, giving up your own claims to the benefit of all.

It is obvious that the aesthetic influence disappears when sexual desire becomes stronger. We come to the conclusion that the aesthetic object triggers instinctual attitudes, but such attitudes are prematurely inhibited and interrupted, so that the aesthetic pleasure, although it offers rest and relaxation, it does not allow a complete satisfaction of desires. Thus, this pleasure continues far from the ideal to be achieved.

The aesthetic object offers a promise and a semi-satisfaction of desires, and such desires are characterized as incompletely satisfied and unfinished by the fact that, in the aesthetic figure, more than a desire seeks expression and satisfaction.

The aesthetic effect consists in the fact that instinctive attitudes are caused, but not developed. That is, the aesthetic experiences are incomplete and can never be completed. The aesthetic object acquires its color when impounding the instinctive energy. The person who appreciates aesthetic experience enjoys the free movement of his desires, without assuming the appropriate responsibility for it.

For Schilder (1935), we should not underestimate the importance of beauty and ugliness in human life. Beauty can be a promise of complete satisfaction or a way to get such satisfaction. Our own beauty or ugliness does not take into account only the image that we have of ourselves, but also the image the others build about us, and which we will take back. Thus, the body image is the result of social life.

Certainly, beauty and ugliness are not isolated individual phenomena, but social phenomena of greater importance. Our own body image and that of others, their beauty or ugliness, become the basis of our sexual and social activities.

For Schilder "the beauty concept is directly related to each people culture" (1935, p. 235). The beauty standard is always the libidinal expression of a society, such as the deformation practices adopted in the primitive societies.

When we structure the individual and others body image, we always tend to build something static that soon will be dissolved again. We always return to the body primary positions. When we think of a person running, we see him changing from a primary position to another primary position. That is, the primary positions are the relative rest position, the moment that the movement is not considered, but yes the postural model crystallized unit.

We should realize that our and others body image is not just a body image at rest, but a body image in motion. But the beauty is especially connected with the body image at rest, with the cover images of certain fashion magazines. And that is why we are so surprised when seeing an isolated phase of a movement in an old photograph

The body image three-dimensionality

Schilder (1935) considers the body as a unit, but points out that to understand the body image, we have to consider the three-dimensional aspect: the world, the body and the mind. He says: "it would be wrong to try to dissolve them in a cluster of isolated parts. We have three categories […] of world, body and personality" (1935, p. 246).

In the construction of body image it is essential the contact with the external reality, because all experiences with external reality already modify the most primitive body image imaginable. Parts of these experiences are accepted or not. Thus, the body image is continuously built through levels and layers, taking into consideration past and present experiences (such as memory and learning).

For Schilder "to build the body image, we need to know where are the different members of our body" (1935, p. 249). The body postural model, the members' knowledge and their mutual relations are necessary to start any movement.

The body postural model finds its expression clearer in the phantom members of people who have lost their members more or less abruptly. An attitude regarding the phantom member shows that people affected with the loss of a member wish to recreate the body integrity. Certain experiments and observations of amputated people show that they contain in themselves the amputated member phantom.

The postural model is modified to each object that touches the body. This model also has relation with the postural model of people around us. In addition, the emotional life has an important role in the final form of body postural model, as it will change the relative value and the clarity of the various parts of the body image, according to the libidinal tendencies.

This change may be a surface change, but also an internal body change. The libidinal structure is expressed in the emphasis given to the different parts of postural model and in appearances resulting from its shapes. What happens in one part of the body can be transposed to another. That is, the female sexual organ cavity can appear as cavity in other parts of the body. The male sexual organ can be represented by earrings, piercings in other parts of the body.

Schilder (1935) calls this a transposition from a body region to another. Therefore, a part of the body can symbolize another part, such as the nose can take the importance of the phallus. Any protruding part can become a symbol of the male sexual organ. The body cavities and orifices can be exchanged by each other freely. The vagina, anus, mouth, ears, and even the nose cavities belong to the same group of orifices.

Conclusion

We elaborate our body image according to the experiences gain through the actions and attitudes, as well as by words or acts directed to our body. In addition, the others attitudes towards their own bodies will also have a major influence on our body image.

We can take other people's body parts and incorporate them into our body image. This is called personalization. Thus, the identification of the group where this subject is inserted, the projection of individual fantasies to the outside world, and the personalization have a prominent role in the construction of an individual body image.

In addition to these three aspects, Schilder also points out that libidinal conflicts constantly change body image. There is a tendency to keep the body image within its bounds, and another to expand and extend it. There is also a tendency to keep their parties united and dissipate them all over the world. So, the movement and the expression belong to destructive phases in the continuous process of changes in the body postural model.

Based on this work, it can be concluded that the erotic changes in body image are always a social phenomena, and followed by the corresponding phenomena in the body image of others. There is a constant exchange between parts of our own body image and the parts of others body image. This means that there is a projection and a personalization. But the others body image totality o (such as friends and neighbors) can be taken in the identification with them; as well as the totality of our body image can be projected to outside.

Therefore, a discussion on body image as an isolated entity is necessarily incomplete. A body is always the expression of an ego, of a personality, and it is inserted into a world. Even a preliminary response to the body problem cannot be given, unless we try a preliminary response on the personality and the world. In other words, for a body image study, any researcher is expected to give prominence to the psychological, physiological and sociological aspects of body image; i.e., its three-dimensionality.

Bibliographical Reference

SCHILDER, Paul (1935/1994). *The Body Image: The Psyche Constructive Energies.* Translation of Rosanne Wertman. São Paulo: Martins Fontes.

The Knives Man: a clinical study

A brief history about the obsessive ritual concept in Freudian theory

The understanding of obsessive ritual on Freudian work presents its first theoretical traces in 1895, in the text *Obsessions and Phobias: its Psychic Mechanism and its Etiology*. Still in the perspective of neurosis traumatic theory, Freud (1895) stated that in obsessions "the original representation [...] was replaced by acts or drives that originally served as relief measures or as protective procedures" (p.169). In these relief measures or protective procedures, the obsessive ritual is found, a symptom considered as a replacement representation of the traumatic event.

During the term of the neurosis traumatic theory (period from 1892 to 1897), Freud (1896) highlights that, in obsessive neurosis, "the subsequent period, the disease, is characterized by the return of repressed memories - that is, by the defense failure" (p. 170). He considers the obsessive ritual as a consequence of the defense failure; that is, as a result of the repressed traumatic memories return. At this time, still under the pillars of neurosis traumatic theory, the obsessive ritual (like other obsessive symptoms) is understood as a compromise formation that represents the repressed return. Consequently, the ego, while repulsing the derivatives of the initially repressed memory (traumatic memory), creates, in this defensive struggle, symptoms that can be classified as secondary defenses, such as the protective actions. These actions include: penitential measures, precautionary measures, oppressive ceremonials, numbers observation, and other actions.

By abandoning the neurosis traumatic theory in 1897, stating that "I do not believe in my neurotic" (letter 69, p. 309),

Freud only returns to the ceremonial act study in 1907, in the text *Obsessive Acts and Religious Practices*.

In this text, Freud (1907) stresses that "the internal understanding of neurotic ceremonial can, by analogy, stimulate us to establish inferences about psychological processes of religious life" (p. 110). He establishes an analogy between the neurotic ceremonial acts and the religious practices: while in neuroses, the instincts nature is exclusively sexual; in religion, these instincts come from selfish sources. The neurotic ceremonial acts are understood as small changes in certain everyday acts, in small additions, restrictions or arrangements that must be performed in the same order. All ceremonial or obsessive acts present an individual character while the religious obsessive acts are carried out in a collective character. In other words, the neurotic ceremonial is carried out as if he was obeying tacit laws. The consciousness that determines its realization, and the anxiety that can arise if something does not go as expected, that grants the ceremonial act its character of sacred act. During the ritual, any interruption can lead the neurotic to certain anguish.

According to Freud (1907), "all details of the obsessive acts have a sense, which serve to important personality interests [...]. They do it in two ways: through direct or symbolic representation and it may, therefore, be historically or symbolically interpreted" (p. 100). That is, the obsessive acts express the obsessive (repressed) wishes, because all obsessive acts details have a sense and can be interpreted. In the rituals, the neurotic symbolically expresses unconscious reasons and ideas.

In addition, the repression failure, pointed out in 1896, is reiterated in this article. For Freud "the repression process that leads to the obsessional neurosis must be regarded as a process that only gets partial success, being constantly under the threat of a failure" (1907, p. 114). In this failure, there are numerous obsessive symptoms, comprising these ceremonial acts.

A good example of obsessive symptom to be mentioned is the case of the young lawyer Ernest Lanzer, the *Rats Man*. In this patient it is the repressed hate towards his father figure (as well as regarding his lady) that motivates him in his rituals. In his protective measures, repressed hostile drives are found; such as the act of removing a stone from the road so that his lady did not have an accident. This protective measure can be considered a symbolic act that expresses all of this patient's unconscious hostility, since moving the stone is an act that neutralizes, annuls the obsessive thinking that something could happen to his lady.

After publishing the clinical case of the *Rats Man*, Freud returns to the study on ceremonial acts in *Totem and Taboo*, in 1913. In this article, while pointing out certain prohibitions present in primitive tribes and comparing them with the neurotic mental life, Freud (1913) postulates that "the most evident and striking concordance pointed between the neurotic obsessive prohibitions and the taboos is that these prohibitions are equally devoid of reason, being similarly mysterious in its origins. Having arisen in certain unspecified moment, they are forcibly maintained by an irresistible fear" (p. 44). Obsessive actions do not have any sense to who practices them. But all ritual is surrounded by a certain conscious fear that any person of the environment may be affected as a result of this ritual breach.

In the obsessive rituals, Freud (1913) says that "the main prohibition, the neurosis nucleus, is against touching him, and hence sometimes it is known as contact phobia or delire du toucher" (p. 45). On obsessive neurotic psychic constitution, any fact or situation that leads his thoughts to the incestuous object is as prohibited as the direct physical contact with the object. And he highlights:

> Obsessive prohibitions involve renunciation and restrictions as extensive in the life of those that are subject to

it as the taboos prohibitions, but some things can be suspended if certain actions were performed […]. These actions […] become compulsive or obsessive acts, and there can be no doubt that they are of the same nature of expiation, penance, defensive measures and of purification [...] The prohibition is loudly conscious, while the persistent desire of touching is unconscious and the subject does not know anything about him" (Freud, 1913, p. 46).

Obsessive acts express the ambivalence present in the neurotic psychic constitution. That is, the desire to touch the incestuous object and the fear to touch it leads the obsessive to an ambivalent attitude regarding the given object. The obsessive constantly wants to perform the touch, but at the same time he fears. The obsessive prohibition is displaced from a ritual to another ritual, covering any new objects and objectives that the forbidden desire can adopt, compensating the repressed instinct.

Freud (1913) ensures that the "obsessive acts begin to be as far as possible of anything sexual – magic defenses against evil desires – and it ends being the substitutes of the forbidden sexual act and the closest possible imitations of it" (p.98). Throughout the obsessive act development, the neurotic is increasingly closer the incestuous act; that is, the prohibited act. In these acts are expressed the ancient romantic and hostile desires that were repressed on the early childhood of this individual. But is should be pointed out that, in all obsessive rituals, the neurotic also expresses the hostile drive, repressed by a prohibition. This repressed drive is always related to some specific act and through the displacement, it is presented through some trivial, commonplace activity of the obsessive.

About the hostility present in obsessive rituals, Freud (1913) also points out that "the hostility is then shut up in the screaming […] by an excessive intensification of affection" (p. 64). As in the case of the *Wolf Man*, who at the age of six had a ritual to breath in a ceremonial manner under certain conditions. This patient, each time he made the cross sign, he undertook to inspire deeply or exhale vigorously. Thus, these acts to expire are related with his paternal identification. This identification becomes a source of intense unconscious hostility, reaching the level of a death desire and a guilt feeling that reacted against this hostility.

On the obsessive ceremonials realization, it is also necessary to highlight the importance of "ruminant" thoughts presence on them. In 1917, in the *Introductory Conferences*, Freud already pointed that the neurotic "undertakes, against his desire, to ruminate thoughts and speculate, as if these were his most important vital problems." (p. 266). It is the presence of ruminant thoughts, drives (such as that of committing serious crimes) and suicide ideas that lead the neurotic to make certain prohibitions, renunciation and restrictions. These ideas, thoughts and drives never come true in acts in reality. Consequently, as he always obtains victory, the escape, and the obsessive precautions, making the obsessive acts very harmless and trivial things, mostly a repetition or ritual elaborations of the individual daily life activities.

After the *Introductory Conferences*, Freud returns to the obsessive ritual theme in 1926, in the text *Inhibitions, Symptoms and Anguish*. In this, he points out that "the erotic-anal components sublimation plays an undeniable role in it [in the obsessive symptom]" (1926, p. 117). In other words, with the child psychic development, the sublimation of the old anal eroticism may be present in certain compulsive rituals of washing the hands and in other obsessive symptoms, and these obsessive rituals are nothing more than mere fruits of certain psychic reactive formations.

According to Freud (1926) "the symptoms that are part of this neurosis fit, in general, into two groups, each having an opposite trend. These are prohibitions, precautions and expiation

[...] or, on the contrary, substitutive satisfactions that often appear in symbolic disguise" (p. 114). The obsessive symptoms formation, such as the obsessive rituals, represents a triumph if they can combine the prohibition with satisfaction. Consequently, the obsessive orders and obsessive prohibitions can provide a certain satisfaction to the obsessive ego. The symptoms (such as the obsessive rituals) are the primary products of obsessional neurosis. These are associated with the activities (which are almost automatically performed) just like going to sleep, bathing and dressing. These tend to repetition and waste of time.

I want to finish this first theoretical part with the reading of André Green about the obsessional neurosis ritual. In the article *Metapsychology of Obsessional Neurosis*, he points out that "the religion – an essentially collective phenomenon - would be here reserved in the exercise of only one [...]" (1967, p.233). This "only one" refers to the individual and solitary character of obsessive ritual, which realization is excluded from the presence of other people. And in the wise words of Green "no neurosis gets to do more than providing the subject, through the symptoms, hidden sources of satisfaction" (1967, p.235-6).

The Knives Man case: A brief approach on the hiding knives ritual.

Before presenting this case, I would like to point out that the source of interest for the obsessive ritual study arises from my unique experience with obsessive patients. In the course of psychotherapy care with these neurotic, at a small public health center, in the countryside of the State of São Paulo, I notice that a large portion of these present some obsessive ceremonial. These always complain of the psychic suffering caused by the daily and compulsive realization of certain ceremonial.

During the care of various obsessive neurotics, I chose a patient that presented a rich obsessive scenario to develop my master's degree research. So, inspired in Freud and his famous clinic case, the *Rats Man*, I decided to name this clinical case of "*The Knives Man*". This fictitious name arises from his ceremonial act of seeking and hiding knives, although, aside from knives, he also hides other objects like scissors, needles and razor blades.

At the beginning of the psychotherapeutic process, the complaints of Claudio, *the Knives Man*, was related to his compulsive thoughts of being "hunting knives". This knife "hunting" means seeking and checking if they are hidden, one in each hole of the wall, the couch, and other places, in which he hid them.

In addition to hiding a knife in each hole in the wall, he also hides razor blades, nails and scissors in lower incidence. He hides a nail into each hole in the wall, but the razor blades and the only scissors in the house; he hides in a kitchen drawer, in which his mother keeps the cutlery.

In his complaints, he also reveals that he cannot stand any longer this search for knives to hide them in his father's toolbox and in the drawer of his wardrobe. He said that he checks, several times, if the knives are hidden, so saying: "these rituals are increasingly making me fatigued [...]. I sleep thinking that there is a knife under my mattress or there in the kitchen [...]. I think that someone could get hurt, but I know that there is no knife there [...]. I wake up and go seek for the blessed. I think that if I do not hunt the knife, I can hurt myself, die, or someone of my family [...]." This someone that may die that he refers, in his later associations, is his father who is described as "rude, angry and who does not take insults from anybody."

This way, Claudio is a young man who comes to psychotherapy marked by his rituals. During our contact, I could know a bit more of his personal history. He declares that he was a quiet and scared child, never getting involved in fights or arguments.

His childhood was market by intestinal problems (constipation crisis), a very present mother and a father always austere. At the age of two and three years, his father worked in the field cutting sugar cane "with a machete". On weekends, the father worked as a cabinetmaker and a barber to earn extra money. Cláudio, at the age of six, presented a constant fear of a possible death of the father figure. And at the age of eight, he began his ritual to hide knives, which lasted throughout his adolescence and current adulthood. Currently, one of his greatest obsessive fears is that the knife, target object of his rituals, comes to poke "his buttocks" if he does not hide it, although he knows that this will never happen.

First of all, for analyzing the ritual of hiding knives, I would like to return, briefly, to two fundamental points of this patient psychic constitution. These two points are:

1st – The constitution of his anal-sadistic phase;

2nd – The possible parental identification present in the pre-genital phases.

The first point, which I believe to be fundamental for the understanding of this obsessive ritual, results from my understanding of how, probably, occurred his anal-sadistic organization. I believe that there might have been a certain fixation of libido during this phase; because in his adult genital organization, he presents various obsessive thoughts which suggest its roots at this phase. He assures: "if the knife thought comes, I hide it because I am also afraid that it pokes me in the buttocks [...]."

So, in this organization, not only the active, sadistic inclination (of retaining faeces) is striking; but also the passivity that left a big mark, since this passivity was fueled by anal eroticism during his remote childhood. The marks of this passivity are one of the keys to the understanding of the fear that a knife could poke him, because this fear (or desire) is based on his old anal eroticism and the repressed negative Oedipus complex, not quitting the relation with the repressed perversion. And recalling that faeces, baby and penis form an unconscious unity, I believe that while fearing that a knife poked him, this obsessive idea seems to represent, symbolically, the desire that the paternal sadist penis penetrated him.

The second point necessary for the understanding of this ritual is the possible paternal identification already present in his pre-genital phases. When Claudio was two and three years old, his father worked in the fields cutting sugar cane; and on weekends, he worked with nails in a small joinery of the ranch where they lived, and he also exercised the profession of barber. I believe that the knives may be representing the father identification, such as the razor blades and the nails too, since they are objects that were used by his father when he worked as a cabinet-maker, country worker and barber during his remote childhood.

The father identification is the central pillar for understanding the emergence of the symptom of hiding knives, at the age of eight. During this ritual, while hiding knives, Cláudio expresses both the identification and all his unconscious hostility to the "father-machete", because of the fact he has interdicted is mother. The identification with the father becomes a source of intense unconscious hostility against him, and the guilt feeling is so striking in the acts of hiding knives that it is also a conscious reaction against this hostility.

At the age of eight, when the act of hiding knives is formed as a protective measure, Cláudio is conscious that he has to hide a knife or someone in his house, like his father, could die. At the beginning of this ritual the ancient parricide desire is expressed, such desire that was barred by the "wolf-caipora" father during his phallic phase and which is manifested, in a symbolic form, in this symptom.

The beginning of the ritual of hiding knives is quite distant from the forbidden act, because it was an inoffensive, banal act, done in silence, and without anyone knowing. Throughout the adult genital organization, this ritual was increasingly approaching the desired act. In other words, the ritual of hiding knives becomes an action that compensates for the realization of the forbidden desire, because the symbolism present in this ritual denotes the prohibited activity: when hiding the knife, he unconsciously wishes, and through an active form, to obtain a pleasure that a day had been banned. And by putting them dirty of butter in his mother's guava sweet or into her washing basing, the patient "reenacts" the desire to have the mother as an object of pleasure, to penetrate her in a sadistic way.

Claudio presents a diversity of places where he hides these objects. I believe that, in each place, he finds a form of substitutionary satisfaction of his unconscious desires, because these desires are displaced into rituals of hiding objects in several different places. These various places where he hides the knives and other objects reflect the overdetermination of this symptom.

Not only this overdetermination is striking in this symptom, but also the use of various defense mechanisms. The first mechanism that is present in this ritual, since he was eight years old, and which will dominate his entire adult psychic life, is the reactive formation mechanism. As the repression failed, the act of hiding knives as a reactive formation against the expected evil emerges; that is, against the fear of his father's death. In this ritual so harmless is already being represented, in a symbolic way, the unconscious hate to the father.

At the age of eight, he also reports that he hid a knife under his bed before going to sleep, because he was afraid that someone of this house could die. He assures: "I went to the kitchen, picked up a knife and put it under my mattress [...]. When I had this thought of knife or death, I used to think or do something else, like hiding knives, to forget this thought [...]. One thought blocked the other."

In saying that he thought or did something to forget the knife thoughts, I believe that another defense mechanism present in this ritual is the displacement. And joint to this mechanism are also present the isolation mechanisms of annulment, because when the knife thought came, he displaced this thought and by means of the act of going to the kitchen, he "annulled" and "isolated" the knife thought, taking and hiding a knife under his bed while he slept on it. In my view, this reveals the presence of the desire of being penetrated by the father, since this act denotes a strategy to try to null the homosexual desire, that is, of obtaining a certain passive pleasure of the paternal penis, of being penetrated by him.

Not only these mechanisms are present in these rituals, but also two other characteristics are striking in the act of hiding knives: the first is the ambivalence presence in the psychic dynamic of this patient; and the second is the presence of a death drive. I take this ambivalence idea from the constant obsessive fear of a possible death of his father, since the fear, the fear that his father died is the result of his defense against the unconscious hate directed to the father figure.

As already mentioned, the second striking characteristic in this ceremonial is the manifestation of the death drive. This means that in this act the destructive drive is being expressed; because, in addition to manifesting all the hostility to his father, he also expresses his destructiveness directed to the external environment.

That is, the knife is a symbolic object that represents, in a contained manner, all destructiveness addressed to the father and to the outside world, but the knife also represents the whole aggressiveness one day introjected in this father, being this knife a representative of the aggressive, sadistic penis introjected by Claudio in his childhood, striking the passage of his passivity (of receiving this penis) for the masculinity, leaving him, forever, handed over the ghost of homosexuality. For this reason the fear of knives also referred to the former homosexual desires of his remote childhood; since the incorporation of this sadistic paternal attribute (currently symbolized by knives) allowed the (dis) pleasure of the identification to his father.

And as the complaint about these rituals permeated our entire clinical contact, I believe that another data still needs to be highlighted in this presentation. Why does he feel so guilt when performing these rituals?

I believe I find the explanations for the guilt feeling in the possible existence of unconscious aggressiveness directed to the father figure. In other words, this guilt is linked, possibly, to the manifestation of the destructive drives in the act of hiding knives.

About this symptom, Claudio also ensures that, after arguing with the father, he passes by each hole checking the knives. In order to relieve himself from the guilt, he gets a knife and hides it. He reports: "when I hide it, it seems that the guilt disappears, strange [...]." While repeating his ceremonial acts, the guilt becomes a vicious circle in the act of hiding knives: at the same time that he relieves from it, it becomes increasingly stronger.

I compare this ritual of hiding knives to a primitive ritual, because each time he sticks a knife in some hole, each time that he symbolically "kills" this dreaded father (who represented an obstacle to his sexual desires), he symbolically satisfies his unconscious hate. But this supposed parricide, that is, this father that symbolically was dead, returns stronger each time due to the old identification of Claudio with him. Consequently, the guilt feeling becomes increasingly intense, and the only possible way for him relieving himself from guilty, as he himself said, is resuming again this act of hiding knives. And, when returning to perform the ritual, he lives what he calls "hell here on Earth [...]. This is a hell; I am paying for my sins still alive [...]."

Beyond the guilt feeling, Claudio presents a very striking animism in his thoughts. He has always believed in mental telepathy, telekinesis, extraterrestrial life, witchcraft and scorcery since his childhood. Another topic that most interests him is related to funeral affairs. During his adolescence, he had a ritual of going to the cemetery and counting the dates that his father's relatives had died. This ritual can be regarded as a manifestation of the parricide desire that one day was present in his infant genital organization. This means that the attitude of going to the cemetery expresses, in a symbolic way, the desire of his father death that was present in the ritual of counting and recounting the numbers of the Batistas' family tombs (fictional surname of this patient father). On the other hand, the act of counting and recounting is a symbolic act of trying to pay the eternal debt with him, for the fact of having desired his death and also of his wife.

I remember the first session he reported this ritual and the association that such memory triggered. This consisted of: "you know, cemetery reminds me death, deceased, dead man [...]." Thus, in his fantasies, Claudio is still stuck to the theme of death. It is his father death, the great figure responsible for his castration, which he attempts to deceive by employing various strategies during his rituals. As a sacred act, he firmly believes that in his rituals, on the strength of his thoughts, in the power and in the realization of his acts of hiding knives, making these his particular region.

On the completion of this succinct clinical interpretation, I would like to point out that the ritual of hiding knives highlights the relationship of a "son-knife" with the "father-machete". In this relation, the paternal identification is revealed since the emergence of Claudio's ritual at the age of eight. During his childhood, while sleeping, he did not have to go around the bedroom with a chair to climb up and kiss religious images hanging on the wall, like the Wolf Man, but he needed to hide a small knife in his bedroom. Currently, during his ceremonial acts, the father is still the big figure that permeates the intricacies of these symptoms, sustained by the (unconscious) hate of this son. Thus, these rituals point to the castrator father figure, which is responsible for the repression of his oedipal desires, causing Claudio to occupy a place never expected by him before. It is about this place that he complains so much during the sessions: the place of a desiring subject, imprisoned by his own repressed desires during his rituals.

Conclusion

On the completion of this article, I want to point out that studying the obsessive ritual does not require only the approach of a ceremony with its repetitive acts. Studying it requires an understanding of the entire psychic dynamic of any obsessive presenting some kind of ceremonial.

In short, this article, by means of a case taken from the care provided at a public health center, reveals that the obsessive ritual, this individual and private religion of the neurotic, is presented through trivial activities of everyday life. In every obsessive act, both the destructive drives, and a desire represented by a counterdesire are being expressed; that is, it is the ambivalence (of desire and fear, love and hate) that surrounds the obsessive ritual execution. And despite the intense psychic suffering, the ritual is approaching more and more of satisfaction and the originally prohibited activity (and eternally desired) of the obsessive.

Bibliographical References

FREUD, Sigmund (1895/1996). **Obsessions and Phobias: its Psychic Mechanism and its Etiology.** ESB, vol. I. Rio de Janeiro: Imago.

_____(1896/1996). **New Comments on the Defense Neuropsychosis.** ESB, vol. III, Rio de Janeiro: Imago.

_____(1897/1996). **Letter 69.** ESB, vol. I, Rio de Janeiro: Imago.

_____ (1907/1996). **Obsessive Acts and Religious Practices.** ESB, vol. IX, Rio de Janeiro: Imago.

_____ (1909/1996). **Notes on a Case of Obsessional Neurosis.** ESB, vol. X, Rio de Janeiro: Imago.

_____ (1913/1996). **Totem and Taboo.** ESB, vol. XIII, Rio de Janeiro: Imago.

_____ (1917/1996). **Conference XVII – The Sense of Symptom.** ESB, vol. XVI, Rio de Janeiro: Imago.

_____ (1918/1996). **History of an Infantile Neurosis.** ESB, vol. XVII, Rio de Janeiro: Imago.

_____ (1926/1996). **Inhibitions, Symptoms and Anguish.** ESB, vol. XX, Rio de Janeiro: Imago.

Green, André (1967). **Metapsychology of Obsessional Neurosis.** In: Psychonévroseobsessionnelleet obsessions (1967). Paris: Encyclopédiemédico-chirurgicale. Translation of Saulo Krieger.

Contemporary reflections on hysterical and obsessive neurosis

Hysteria: A brief articulation on the contemporary symptomatic manifestations in the Brazilian context

Among the classes of neurosis studied by Sigmund Freud, the conversion hysteria can be considered the hysterical neurosis itself. This neurosis is side by side to the obsessional neurosis and the anxiety hysteria – the phobia – which wealth was 'hushed up' by the famous Panic Syndrome.

Among these three classes of neurosis – the obsessive, phobic and the hysterical -, the conversion hysteria was the precursor to the psychoanalysis origin. In his early studies, Freud did not use the 'conversion hysteria terminology, since the 'conversion' terminology was considered as a hysteria itself. In this conversion, the psychic drive, interlaced to the desire, is bodily manifested through contractions, blindness and other symptoms, but it was on the analysis of a phobia case – the little Hans – that the father of psychoanalysis began to discern between the anguish hysteria (with all its clinical richness that the famous psychiatry confined it) and the conversion hysteria.

In the thresholds of this historical trajectory, between the pre-psychoanalysis and the analysis of little Hans, the conversion hysteria and its clinical manifestations were never relegated to a second plan. In this historic meander, the historian Roudinesco (1988) points out that, between 1880 and 1900, the world was going through a real epidemic of hysterical symptoms, being these understood by doctors, historians and writers as the convulsive signs of female nature as a result of the industrial society consequence in the 19th century.

This time Jean Martin Charcot is highlighted, a French physician and neurologist, who understood the hysteria as a functional and hereditary disease, which affected men and women. Through the hypnosis, he tried to demonstrate his assumptions on this pathology.

This technique was widely used with his patients of Salpêtrière, inducing to his hysterical symptoms. This doctor, to whom Freud had a huge consideration, directly influenced the psychoanalysis father understandings on hysteria. Between 1888 and 1893, Freud brings from Charcot the idea in which the hysterical neurosis is a result of a childhood trauma, reporting that his would have its sexual causes and would be the result of a sexual abuse really lived by the child during his childhood.

Due to his self-analysis in 1897, he waives this theory and emphasizes the role of fantasy in the hysteria etiology. In the passage to the 20th century, the psychoanalysis technique suffers a new change: Freud abandons the cathartic method of Breuer - a method which psychoanalytic therapy was based on the treatments carried out by hypnosis. In this method, through hypnosis, the patient came into contact with the traumatic events, releasing the emotions related to him.

In contrast, Freud adopts the free association, focusing the verbalized material freely throughout the sessions. This method, according to Laplanche (2001), would insist in indiscriminately expressing the thoughts freely from the childhood memories, reports of dreams and the symptoms brought by the patient.

At the turn of the century, in 1900, Freud writes *The Dreams Interpretation*, the book which is considered the landmark of the beginning of psychoanalysis. In this context, hysteria was understood as a psychic conflict and no longer as a result of a traumatic event. There the hypnosis had been abandoned and the free association method gains its space.

Before proceeding, I would like to highlight that, although 114 years have passed from the hypnosis technique abandonment, this, in our Brazilian current society, gains space between charlatan 'professionals', which use it in favor of their primitive religious rituals. We are no longer in Salpêtrière and the hysterics are no longer put on stage; but the stage was transformed into the television and the internet, which give room for the collective alienation that moves a mass in the search of an answer to the others suffering. A reply in the search for nothing, moved by the desire; such as the primitives that beat their drums in the search for an answer from their loved superior for the pain of their soul. Therefore, we observe the suffering of a mass in which many, by the scientific ignorance, put, often, the salvation in people who they shamelessly use, and without the ethical pillar, the distortions of hypnosis technique to justify the failures and the diseases of this crowd, evoking the evil beings within these people. So we return to middle ages, because all that is wrong is not our fault, but the punishments of superior beings that we should exorcise.

In this meander, hysteria never was made so clamored in our society. But before proceeding, I would like to point out that we cannot equate hysteria to madness, like many still do, repeating the mistakes of our past. I hear many saying that the hysteric is a crazy woman that screams, kicks and shows up. But it is not. On the contrary, if the show occurs, this is of her own desire that circulates and moves the dissatisfaction of her own psychism. So if hysteria puts in evidence the desire and we owe them the psychoanalysis origin, we will return to Freud, specifically until 1901, when Freud wrote the classic case of hysteria: *the Dora case.*

In this clinical case, he considered hysteric "any person in which an opportunity of sexual excitement provokes [...]a sensation of disgust, whether that person presents or not somatic symptoms" (1901, p. 50). However, it was after the studies on infant sexuality that Freud indicated the core of hysterical neurosis: this would be in the impossibility to liquidate the Oedipus

complex (nuclear complex of the psychic subject constitution).
Such statement requires a better explanation.

All of us, human beings, entered in the Oedipus complex, but how each one dealt with the destinations of this complex only an analysis can point out. In this meander, according
to the Freudian theory, the female Oedipus complex does not
occur similar to the male, since in the female path of this complex, the penis envy comes to perform a key role. In this case,
the girl enters this complex by the discovery that not all feature
a male organ. In this turmoil, she disconnects from the mother
– since this deprived her from the male organ – In the search of
her father, expressing the desire to have a son with him, which
in the past she desired to have from her mother. Thus, all female
Oedipus complex entire development is concrete in the penile
envy shadow. However, it is the fear of the maternal love loss
that throws the girl 'out' of this complex, and the girl may show
three possible escapes: the sexual inhibition or hysteria, the masculinity complex and the femininity.

As the female hysteria is presented as possible it exist
to the female Oedipus complex, it is the libidinal fixation in
the phallic phase that will move it in its eternal complaints of
dissatisfaction. In other words, among the three phases of psychosexual development described by Freud – the oral, anal and
phallic – the hysteria features a great part of the libidinal fixation
in the phallic phase, a phase that culminates with the Oedipus
complex. In contrast, if this phallic fixation was not enough,
there is also a small fixation on oral phase, which justifies why
many hysterical have such strong melancholic traits. Therefore,
it was this world so rich and enigmatic of female universe that
surprised Freud at each phase of his work.

However, I point out that every hysterical will move according to these fixations, assuming, in each case, a unique position against its transference. So the psychotherapists are respon-

sible for hearing them, always being attentive of their fantasies (and not the reality) in their verbalizations.

Those fantasies that launch new light on the manifestations of its libidinal fixations: each hysterical moves by the phallus (or its lack), leading her to claim prominent places and positions in society, putting in checkmate the male positions and jobs. This means that the hysterical complaint, which reflects this phallic position and that still moves many women, is very common when they assume roles and positions below the men. Such difference can never end, because it is this what drives her desire, given the lack. And in the completeness pursuit of this lack, a fact that she can never show, the hysterical is capable of great facets, these being of great social recognition.

Here I would like to point out a book called *Everything in Pink*, written by the own hands of the arts godmother of São Paulo, the great Yolanda Penteado. In my understanding, this author, at the same time that describes her own story, brings the issue of love of her childhood in relation to her parents, as well as the good identificatory relation with her mother, pointing to the life force that was present in her psychic constitution. When getting aware of her love frustrations and how she stood up in view of her personal conflicts, Yolanda portrays how love and seduction were part of her daily life. To compensate this lack of phallus, she lived directly with phallic men, such as Santos Dumont (to whom she refused numerous times the marriage invitation), but came to marry, after her divorce, with Ciccillo Matarazzo, one of the Brazil's most influential men in the 50s. In the 1920 and 1930 decades, she was present in the female claims for the equal vote, since this was a right only of men. She was also present, with Anita Malfatti and TarsilaAmaral, in the Modern Art week, in the decade of 1920. Let us see: influential women that made history; but her greatest wealth was the MASP – Art Museum of São Paulo – opened in the decade of

1950. Thus, her life was marked by works that brought the phallic glow to her person. A bright that was portrayed with plenty of life in the book mentioned above.

Examples aside, I would like to return to a point of hysteria: The body symptoms. Roudinesco (1998) points out that the originality of this neurosis lies in the fact that her unconscious psychic conflicts are expressed from a theatrical way through body symbolizations, such as the attacks or convulsion in epileptic appearance, paralysis, contractures and other symptoms. Among these, a feature that catches my attention is the seduction, moved by the desire.

In hysteria, due to the phallic fixation, a triangulation is formed, where many serious hysterical are put as the third in the relationship. When they are called by the partner to assume a serious relationship, as a couple, such pleasure is lost. Consequently the desire starts to move in search of relationships that refer again to this triangulation, decoding its identificatory problematic. I remember a hysterical saying: "I was not born to be a woman; I was born to be a lover, the other, only that". Such relationships put in evidence the rivalry with the mother in the search of the father and that, in the adulthood, it is incorporated, respectively, by the lover and the lover wife. Therefore, the seduction becomes the main weapon, but falling in its claws is everything that the hysterical least wants, but desires. And in this psychic conflict, hysteria moves in the meanders of modern society.

Due to this, the popular judgments label them of numerous derogatory names, repeating the lack of knowledge about this pathology. If before, the hysteria was decoded as demonic possession, since the witches put in checkmate the male phallus and the religion phallus, currently, the hysteria acquires even more force, because the hysterical dispute the society hypocrites pillars through the pan protests in public square, but her demands for better wages, etc. The inquisition of fires no longer exists, but they are burned in the inquisitions that exist within each one of us when we contest what cannot be contested: the female independence. That is why this neurosis will never be outdated.

Contemporary manifestations of obsessional neurosis: A clinical reflection

Today we live in a society in which the famous psychiatric classifications are present even in the conversation circles among friends. In the coming and going of the day to day complaints, who never suspected that was experiencing depression or phobias? Within this macro context, there is a micro context that needs a special look: the clinic, the space in which the psychotherapist bends himself on the history of each patient, trying to understand them in the context where each one is inserted. In the meanders of these 'modern pathologies' that move the intense and famous company of pharmaceuticals, it is still very common to hear from many patients, in the first sessions, that they suffer from the Panic Syndrome or that they are full of cleaning manias. Many associate this manias with the famous T.O.C; i.e., with the obsessive compulsive disorder.

This disorder, present in the psychiatry manuals as an anxiety disorder, was compared to the obsessional neurosis. Such comparison is a big mistake; since this compendium does not consider the uniqueness of Freudian discoveries made by the father of psychoanalysis at the turn of the 19th century until his last writings. This means that we cannot compare the obsessive compulsive disorder to the advances of the studies on obsessional neurosis, both Freud and also the post-Freudian, where we find the British psychoanalyst Melanie Klein and the French psychoanalyst Jacques Lacan. While the obsessional neurosis presents a plurality of clinical manifestations, considering the unique story of each patient, the obsessive compulsive disorder only focus on the symptomatic manifestations.

Here a dilemma arises: the obsessive symptomatic manifestations of this disorder does not necessarily belong to the obsessional neurosis, since the differential diagnosis of psychotherapists of psychoanalytic approach support in the infant desires manifestations of these neurotic; that is, all and every obsessional neurosis diagnosis is based on the transfer of childhood complexes, where the anal drives of infant sexuality keep its proper importance. While the psychotherapist observed and heard the history manifestations of each patient that underlies behind this neurosis, many psychiatrists still focus only in the obsessional symptomatic manifestations for their diagnosis, not considering the infant desires and the drives that are spread behind these symptoms.

As we are inserted in a society where the American pragmatism still perpetuates, many psychologists (and other health professionals) still criticize the psychoanalytic psychotherapies, signaling that these are long and little effective. This criticism deserves reflections: if, on one hand we have this posture that refers us to the 19[th]century, on the other, this neurosis, which begins between six and eight years, deserves a resumption in Freudian work. In other words, if the obsessional neurosis is not the obsessive compulsive disorder, what would this neurosis be then? Let us resume briefly the Freudian studies.

Freudian conception

The obsessional neurosis owes (and a lot) to Sigmund Freud studies, the psychoanalysis mentor. His early studies on this neurosis are dated 1894, when he wrote the text *The Psychoneurosis of Defense*, breaking with the classical psychiatry vision and demarcating, according to the psychoanalyst Hayat (2005), that this neurosis had as an origin a intrapsychic conflict of sexual origin that mobilized and blocked all the energies of the individual. Thus, since the end of the 19th century, next to the hysteria, the obsessions began to gain the look of Freud, once he noted that in the etiology of obsessions classic symptoms – such as the doubts, guilt and rituals – there was a psychosexual component; in other words, a component of sexuality linked to the psychic.

After having written two books that put in check the Cartesian thinking of his time – *The Dreams Interpretation* (in 1900) and the *Three Essays On the Infant Sexuality* (in 1905) – Freud resumed the study on the obsessional neurosis in a short article titled *Obsessive Acts and Religious Practices*, published in 1907. In this, he compares the obsessive rituals to the devout acts, being the obsessive rituals moved by the individual desires of each neurotic. However, this context requires a special attention: ten years before, in 1897, due to his self-analysis, Freud abandoned the traumatic theory of neuroses.

This theory understood that the obsessional neurosis would be the result of a sexual abuse not penetrated by a pervert adult in the childhood of these patients. Due to his self-analysis, the psychoanalysis father understood that the complaints that persisted behind the reports of these patients came from their fantasies and not from the reality experienced by them.
It was in these fantasies (and not in reality) that the sexual content was present. So, Freud begins to observe the fantasies behind the neurotic symptomatology, leading him to abandon this theory. Later, Freud resumes the studies on obsessions in 1907, when writing the article *Obsessive Acts and Religious Practices*. In this meander, the psychoanalysis father was already analyzing the case of Ernst Lanzer, the famous clinical case that became known as the Rats Man.

Lanzer suffered from obsessions that rats could penetrate him by the anus. Such obsessions were triggered after hearing the Lieutenant of his army report of an oriental torture technique. In this technique, according to Roudinesco (1998), the prisoner was forced to undress and to kneel on the floor, and on his buttocks was fixed, by means of a belt, a large perforated bowl through which a rat was agitating. When trying to escape, this rat could penetrate into the rectum of the begged, inflicting him bloody wounds.

This idea afflicted him so much that he himself sought Freud due to his ruminant and punitive thoughts with the rats. Therefore, because of these obsessions, this patient became known as the *Rats Man*, becoming the first classic case of obsessional neurosis in the history of psychoanalysis.

When publishing this case in 1909, Freud arouses the clinical attention for the entire obsessive symptomatology that translated the ambivalence between the love and hate of this patient. His obsessions reflected his anal drives, from his childhood.

But it was in 1913, when writing *The Inclination to Obsessional Neurosis*, that Freud pointed out the relevance of the anal-sadistic phase and the anal eroticism for the understanding of the obsessive symptomatology. Let us remember that Freud described three phases of human psychosexual constitution: the oral phase (of external world incorporation through the mother milk suction), the anal-sadistic phase (where we find ambivalences surrounded by the faeces game), and the phallic phase (where culminates the Oedipus complex – the unconscious representation by which the amorous and hostile desires of children are expressed towards his parents).

Freud, in this text of 1913, stresses the importance of the anal sadistic phase for the understanding of obsessional neurosis symptomatology, since the regression of libido – of sexual energy – to this phase is the predisposition to understand the events that occur in this neurosis. Thus, we find in the anal-sadistic phase the pillars that guide the movements of these neurotics. But how can we identify them?

It is very common, in adulthood, that these neurotic present a supermorality, a super kindness, such as an inclination to order and harmony. Such features are defenses against the dirty, anal, drives present in their unconscious. But between the meanders of clinic and the social, the obsessional neurosis brings something that is missing in the current Brazilian society: the inclination to order, hierarchy – given by the relationship with the father – and the issue of the work. This is the inheritance of the symptomatic positivity of this pathology, which many researchers cannot see. While many are dealing with the obsessive symptoms through a negative lens, creating pathologies for everything and everyone that show manias and rituals, the positivity of this neurosis brings features that break with these stereotypes. But which would they be?

Among the guilty, the rituals and the attachment to time and money – characteristics that refer, directly or indirectly, to the anal-sadistic phase – the obsessive neurotic makes the work of the springboard for the (dis)pleasure of his daily life, leading the secondary benefits of this 'symptom' until the structuring of his daily life. So, these neurotics have the work, religion and the family as the triad that regulates his behavior and his judgments.

If we analyze the history of each one in its uniqueness, even in their threshold, this neurosis reveals a richness of demonstrations that goes since the primitive thinking form – where we find the superstitions – up to the relationship with the father, being this a representative of the law that the obsessive incorporates and transmits throughout the generations. His ruminant, tragic or banal thoughts are evoked and softened over its rituals: in these, the father figure is always evoked by the guilt that drives these neurotics in their eternal beliefs, like for example, once a patient reported me that if he did not hide the scissors of his house, his father could die. And in his prayers, he begged for his father constant protection. This excerpt demonstrates the ambivalence of this obsessive patient.

Among so many manifestations, the religious devotion is another trademark of these patients, driven by guilt. This fact had already been observed by Freud in 1907, in the text already mentioned, and numerous times reintegrated throughout his work, mainly in *Totem and Taboo*, published in 1913.

In this text, when comparing the primitive minds with the mind of these neurotics, the psychoanalysis father had already highlighted the belief in the superstitions and in thought power can be highlighted in this pathology. As the Rats Man had already been analyzed in 1909, Freud reiterates that in this neurosis, the regression of acting for thinking was evident. In other words, the great (dis)pleasure is in rumination of thoughts that symbolically evidence the desires of these patients. The thought comes to replace the act itself, leaving them given to inaction, i.e., the lack of attitude due to the ambivalent conflict in his psyche. For this reason these patients spend hours and hours ruminating tragic thoughts of death of a loved one who, many times, refers to the old parricide desires of his own childhood.

In this ambivalence, between the desire and the fear, we can also find love hiding the hatred of the same intensity, or even an intense morality and an attachment to cleaning which leads him to develop cleaning or purification rituals. Such rituals became a mere defense of anal-erotic drives that persist in his unconscious. The pursuit for cleaning hides a dirt that, unconsciously, refers to the idea of the faeces and to his disorganization. Everything that the neurotic can never demonstrate.

In addition, the defense mechanisms present in this neurosis were the subject of Freud study since the clinical case of the Rats Man; but it was in *Inhibitions, Symptoms and Anxiety* (from

1926) that Freud addresses a chapter to his latest discoveries of mechanisms in this neurosis. Among these, we have the isolation (in which, according to Laplanche, such mechanism consists in isolating a through in such a way that the remaining connections with other thoughts are interrupted), the annulment (in which an act or action negates the first, using a thought or behavior with an opposite meaning), the displacement (of an aggressive act to an anal act), and the reactive formation, being this an attitude or habit of totally opposite sense to the repressed desire, constituting a reaction against it.

Among all these manifestation, unique in each verbalized history, we cannot forget that in the neurosis class, specifically the obsessive, the society standard and rules are perpetuated, even if for this, it pays high price for its symptom. In a society in which the right rests to the perverse and the duties to the neurotic, the obsessive neurosis survives in the middle of a social holocaust.

However, among its many clinical riches, this neurosis proposes a reflection on the order and law structuring. If this breaks the paternal conflicts, as many psychoanalysts point out, it is from this conflict that results a doubt that organizes the society into an order movement, structuring the rules that govern the good habits. From the fragility of this law is that we can notice the perverse movements, which lead young people and adults to commit barbarous acts. That is why the search for justice is present in the context and in the verbalization of this neurosis.

Psychiatry and reductions

Finally, I would like to return to the beginning of this paper and refute the idea that any psychopathology must be diagnosed by the symptoms. For this purpose, it would be interesting to return to Melanie Klein, the 'mother' of British psychoanalysis. Although this psychoanalyst is criticized by the psychoanalysts of the French current, I mean the Lacan followers, such criticisms are supported in a prejudice without justification, once the theory proposed by her opens the doors for the psychotic patients analysis while the Lacan followers, when analyzing Klein work, pored in intellectual criticism of narcissist nature. Quarrels and rivalries aside, I should mention the Klein brought a new vision to the obsessive symptomatology.

This psychoanalyst points out that all and any obsessive symptom is in the defense of possible psychotic centers. Thus, the symptom becomes a defense and not the cause of a pathology. And it is from this that it really scares me to observe psychoanalysts adopt a symptomatology posture and persist in errors that culminated in the history tamponment of these patients. This means that not every obsessive symptoms refers, unique and exclusively, to a case of obsessional neurosis. For this reason that we live with a 'salad' of diagnostics.

An exit for this 'chaos' would be the listening, a listening without prejudices and above any intellectual judgment. A listening marked by the clinical observation and by patient manifestations and associations in the clinical setting. Only this way we can understand the plurality of this neurosis, manifested in the uniqueness of each patient.

Conclusion

The discussions above show that both neuroses – hysterical and obsessive – put in check the manifestations of desire that interlace with drive inclinations in our society. While the hysterical neurosis puts in evidence the phallic fixation, moving the hysteria in favor of the phallic bright manifestation and the social recognition in its productions, the obsessional neurosis proposes the freezing logic of thoughts and actions, denoting that these manifestations bring, to the foreground, the characteristics of the self-destructive drive. These two classes of neurosis are self-complemented: one moved by the drive of life and the other by the drive of death; but as in any case there is an exception, for each class of neurosis there is a lack that cannot be completed by plenitude: there comes the symptom, glittering the desire in its manifestations in the pursuit of the eternal completeness that will never be achieved, moving these two classes of neuroses in the tamponment of what cannot be covered, shut up what cannot be silent: the desire and its manifestations in the pursuit of the childish desire eternally lost, but always idealized. Welcome to the neurotic family.

Bibliographical Reference

HAYAT, M. (2005). Obsessional Neurosis. In: Mijola, Alain de.*International Dictionary of Psychoanalysis.*Translation of Álvaro Cabral. Rio de Janeiro: Imago.

FREUD, S. (1894/1996). The Defense Psychoneurosis.*ESB*, vol. III, Rio de Janeiro:Imago.

_____. (1900/1996). The Dreams Interpretation. *ESB*, vol. V, Rio de Janeiro: Imago.

_____. (1905/1996). Fragment of the Analysis of a Hysteria Case. *ESB*, vol. VII.Rio de Janeiro: Imago.

_____. (1907/1996). Obsessive Acts and Religious Practices. *ESB*, vol. IX.Rio de Janeiro:Imago.

_____. (1909/1996). Notes on a Case of Obsessional Neurosis. *ESB*, vol. X. Rio de Janeiro:Imago.

_____. (1913/1996). The Inclination to Obsessional Neurosis

– A Contribution to the Problem of Neurosis. *ESB*, vol. XII.Rio de Janeiro:Imago.

_____. (1923/1996). The Infant Genital Organization: an Interpolation of Sexuality Theory. *ESB*, vol. XIX, Rio de Janeiro:Imago.

_____. (1925/1996). Some Psychic Consequences of Anatomical Distinction Between the Sexes. *ESB*, vol. XIX, Rio de Janeiro:Imago.

_____. (1926/1996). Inhibitions, Symptoms and Anxiety. *ESB*, vol. XX, Rio de Janeiro:Imago.

_____. (1933/1996). XXXIII Conference - Femininity. *ESB*, vol. XXII, Rio de Janeiro:Imago.

LAPLANCHE, J. & PONTALIS, J-B.(1967/2001). *Psychoanalysis Vocabulary.* São Paulo: Martins Fontes.

PENTEADO, Yolanda (1976). *Everything in Pink.* Rio de Janeiro: Nova Fronteira.

ROUDINESCO, Elisabeth & PLON, Michel (1998). *Psychoanalysis Dictionary.* Rio de Janeiro: Jorge Zahar editor.

French psychoanalyst Piera Aulagnier concept about the neurosis psychopathology

From her clinical practice with psychotic patients, Piera Aulagnier develops the potentiality concept to replace the term "structure" proposed by Jacques Lacan. When writing her book *The Interpretation Violence*, she states: "the psychotic potentiality is [...] a psyche organization that cannot product manifested symptoms" (1970, p. 177). Before writing about this work, her productions were directed, among other issues, to the maniac-depressive structure, the psychotic structure and the perverse structure. With this book publishing in 1975, this distinguished psychoanalyst replaces the term structure by potentiality. Although she does not make a concept, at that moment, of what would be the potentiality, she only states that this would be a psychic potentiality, which could remain latent or the psychosis can arise from this. Thus, Aulagnier understands that the potentiality concept is related with something virtual, in potential, due to a psychic inclination determined in childhood, in a definition quite close to the psychic inclination approached by Freud.

In 1984, when writing *The Historian Apprentice and the Wizard Master*, Aulagnier understands that potentiality concepts "include the 'possible' I functioning and its identificatory positions, once childhood is finished" (1989, p.228). Aulagnier understands the potentiality concept as an indentificatory position that 'I' will assume at the end of childhood. This means that it is at T2 point where potentiality can be established, deciding on the response and defense ways that 'I'can have when confronted with a conflict. Thus, it is at this moment (T2), at the moment of the conclusion time, with the assumption (or not, or partial) of castration, that the neurotic potentiality, psychotic or polymorphic definitely settles, unless the autism or a psychosis appears in childhood.

For Aulagnier "the psychopathological phenomena totality, which we find in the clinical practice in various forms, are the more or less disguised consequence and manifestation operating at the level of the "I" investments and, therefore, in his identificatory economy" (1985, p.18). Aulagnier understands the potentiality as identificatory conflicts, comparing the identificatory building with a puzzle. This means that when making use of a metaphor, Aulagnier points out that this puzzle fittings must be the certitude points in which the child "I" will anchor. These certitude points were provided by the identified present in the parental discourse, such as the maternal, so prevalent. To these certitude points the identificants are added and by which the child is named; first, appropriating the parental discourse, to subsequently, getting certain independence.

The (un)fittings and the identificatory conflict

For a better understanding of such fittings, Aulagnier emphasizes that it "is effectively the identificant relation with these certitude points present in the identified that makes it possible and preserves the symbolic identification" (1985, p. 23). For prolonging the discussion on the identificatory building idea, I would like to point out that, for Aulagnier , the zero type (T^0) is related to the baby birth, with the primary identification, extending until time one (T1), at the 'I' institution moment through the imaginary or speculate identification. This time - T1- marks the beginning of a new identificatory journey, extending until the time two (T2), the time to conclude, when it is expected that the symbolic identification occurs, leading to the project identification. By means of infantile sexuality repression, the castration assumption leads to the 'I' reshaping in terms of identificatory position, causing the puzzle pieces re-fittings. This means that, at the first set of fittings which constitute the certitude points in which 'I' had anchored, other pieces are joint, which emblems consider the expected image and invested by the look of the demands recipients, adapting to the first fittings.

Regarding such fittings, Aulagnier states:

> Before approaching the 'identificatory conflict' […], we consider, through an artifice, the identificant-identified relation, regardless the function the identificatory aspiration occupies […]. The image that is sent from I to his own retina and the others retina is, jointly, the enunciation that he provides to these two images [...]. What returns to the I as the identified that represents him, will always be different from what he expects from this present moment, in which his aspirations of yesterday materializes. And in this difference one cannot forget the role that […] a mourning, a disappointment [...] will have and which can affect the I (1985, p. 25-26).

This heterogeneous characteristic of 'I' is responsible for the conflict potentiality. This means that the weakness points of this fittings between identificant-identified, the unfitting risks and the gap between these pieces, will always be present. If this conflict occurs between the first group and the pieces added that unveil what 'I' is becoming, or has become, here we have a neurotic potentiality, a moment in which the conflict will occur between 'I' and his ideals, causing the neurotic conflict. Thus, by understanding the potentiality as identificatory conflicts, this psychoanalyst brings new conceptions of psychopathology, where we find the psychotic potential, (in which the identificatory conflict occurs inside the 'I', between his identified and identificant dimensions), the neurotic potentiality and the polymorphic potentiality (in which we have the conflict between 'I' and his ideals and inside 'I').

The neurotic conflict

About the neurotic conflict, Aulagnier states:

> While the conflict respects the identificant-identified unit to oppose 'I' and his ideals, its consequences will be less dramatic. The conflict, in this case, will be the identificatory aspirations coexistence, contradictory, that is, the contradiction between the current 'I' and what he wants or prohibits to become: this conflict is the neurosis (1985, p. 26).

Aulagnier, postulating that in the neurotic potentiality there is a conflict between 'I' and his Ideals, she does not exclude the conflict between instances, neither the impulsive conflict, as it is described by Freud, but points out that this conflict chronicity and intensity that specifies the neurotic commitment. So, over the course of her work, by agreeing with Freud conceptions on neurosis, her methodological and technical reflections become as a reference to the neurosis clinic, although she continues contributing to the other psychopathologies, including psychosis.

Aulagnier adds that, on neurotic potentiality, the "conflict concerns the investments between 'I' and the objects which it demands 'a plus' pleasure" (1985, p. 138). This means that the investment in ideals is not a vital requirement, but it is necessary, at certain moments, so this 'I' chooses to live.

About the neurosis, she points out:

> Every neurosis has its manifested form the moment
> in which an Oedipus complex should be dissolved, the
> moment in which the investment directed to the paren-
> tal Selves should not disappear, but modify through a
> demand decantation to them directed and through the
> desire to find new recipients to the demands that can no
> longer be addressed to the parents. Repression which al-
> lows 'I' forget that he expected from the parents a sexual
> pleasure, when in fact he preserves such desire thanks to
> the determination that is operated […] (1985, p. 161).

In neurosis there is an impulsive investment of 'I' in an
expanded reality represented by a space that goes beyond the
family space. The investment in a new object, in a new 'I', can
only come true, without a larger conflict, if 'I' feels confident of
an agreement between this new 'I' and the ideal representations
already invested in his past and which he cannot abandon or
modify. This means that, in this extended reality, in the neurosis
field, we can find an old demand that was addressed to the parents being aimed at new people, although there is 'I' ignorance
about the sexual component neurotic included in this demand
to his replacements. So, the answer the neurotic receives from
this demand cannot satisfy what it is covered behind the appar-
ent legitimacy of pleasures that this 'I' conjectures to ask.

In relation to this reply intended for other people, Aulagnier also falls back to repression failure, pointing out:

> The neurotic symptomatology blooms when 'I' in-
> vested the 'I' of another because he thought so to satisfy
> his childhood demand, what proves that he only changed
> the recipient, without then modifying what he expected
> in response to his first demands: to be loved, protected, as

he wanted to be loved and protected by his parents and, moreover, that give him sexual pleasure (1985, p. 161).

On neurosis, the demand addressed to another becomes utopian, because the other cannot be, at the same time, mother and sexual partner, as well as the father cannot become his lover, and the son (or daughter) his pleasure object. All this happens thanks to the repression effect. Thus, the neurotic symptomatology will manifest when 'I' invests in another 'I' because he wanted to be loved and protected, willing to satisfy his former childish demand, but thanks to the repression effect, this sexual pleasure becomes impossible.

For Aulagnier "by the neurosis side, T2 matches the assumption by 'I' of a symbolic position that he can preserve and respect" (1989, p.234). At this point, the neurotic conflict lies in the imaginary registry and the aggregated pieces choice. This means that the neurotic continues to project on his successive identified the shadow of that, which is supposedly the only one who can attract into his advantage a love that he could repeat the same love expected and required in his remote childhood, but due to repression (secondary), such fact cannot be conceived.

For this psychoanalyst, the secondary repression goal is "to exclude from the 'I' space certain impulsive representations which representation is incompatible with cultural requirements that cannot be infringed, and with identificatory positions that are the only ones that can allow the 'I' to perform a portion of his desires, his demands, and his goals" (1989, p. 267). Due to this secondary repression, we found the incest and patricide interdict. This means that the interdictions pronounced by the parental instance became a megaphone of cultural requirements. These interdicts are already present in the parents repressed, i.e., in the desire to which they renounced in their remote childhoods.

Aulagnier points out that "in the neurosis registry, the suffering essential cause the presence of a desire that we cannot or that we interdict to perform, at the same we refuse to renounce it" (1990, p. 296). In the neurosis, as desire is related to oedipal object, its resignation is seen by the neurotic as the eventual disappearance of all desire. Consequently, the neurotic transformed into suffering cause a child investment and it still remains as a source of pleasure. Therefore, preserving the investment in other people, the neurotic creates a false illusion of his suffering disappearance.

This suffering, to Aulagnier, "protects the subject of a persecutory relationship" (1990, p. 228). It is the system itself and the neurotic commitment to adopt the suffering of a relational function in which we find his non-sharing , imposing to the neurotic, what Aulagnier calls the "absolute solitude experience" (1990, p. 298). And it is in this solitude experience that many obsessive neurotics keep their obsessive thoughts, their secret rituals and other symptoms, under lock and key.

But after all, how does this distinguished psychoanalyst understands the neurotic symptom concept? Aulagnier defines neurotic symptom as "a compromise between the repression and the 'I' repressor action, after a first failure, that tries to control what returns, and creates a barrier that protected him against this irruption" (1985, p. 17). That is, the neurotic symptomatic construction refers to the identicatory conflict existing in the space between 'I' and his ideals. So, it is this conflict chronicity, present in the neurotic symptom, which will specify the neurosis intensity.

According to Aulagnier "whatever the neurotic symptomatology is, its center always reveals an identificatory conflict. It is proper to the neurotic 'I' to be taken by an unsustainable doubt concerning his truth and his affections" (1990, p. 236). This quote matches this thesis problematic. Namely, when pointing that in all neurotics symptomatic center there is an identificatory conflict, Aulagnier points out an intrinsic relation between symptomatic formation and the identificatory problem. In addition, here I highlight the importance given to the neurotic symptomatology doubt, since 'I' is already sentenced to doubt and not to fall into the certitude abyss.

If the ability to doubt is linked to the thinking activity, Aulagnier points out that the neurotic "can [...] preserve the thought functioning, preserve creativity and the resulting pleasures, and, often, super invest this pleasure" (1985, p. 161). It is in the neurotic pathologies that the thinking and investing functions are compromised, and the right to choose the thoughts that communicate and those which he keeps secret is a vital condition for the 'I' proper functioning.

In the neurosis "having to think, having to doubt the thought, having to check it; these are requirements to which 'I' cannot avoid, the price at which he pays his citizenship right in the social field and his participation in the cultural adventure" (Aulagnier, 1990, p. 271). The 'I' learned quickly that thinking is a necessary work and comprises many evidences, causing pleasure and displeasure. So, think and invest denominate two functions without which the 'I' could not accrue, or preserve his space in the psychic scene, and the suffering, displeasure, is the price that they should pay for his existence.

For Aulagnier "the neurotic will actually have the inclination, during the session, to mainly invest 'transference thoughts', he will rarely think of a 'pink cloud' by the sole pleasure of his having this thought" (1900, p. 277). And the neurotic subject 'I' should be able to oppose his pleasure or displeasure right inalienability about certain thoughts, determining his right to secretly think and experience pleasure or displeasure with it. Remember that a necessary condition to the 'I' functioning is present in the fact that he could exercise his right to think and enjoy on his own thought activity. On neurosis, even if the thinking freedom is not unlimited, all its forms are characterized by a partial loss of that thought freedom due to the repression action. Consequently, the exclusion of a number of thoughts becomes possible at the expense of 'I' thought activity impoverishment, of a loss of power to think without locks. Thus, we find here one of the neurotic suffering reasons: the intellectual inhibition.

Beyond the intellectual inhibition, on neurosis, the subject can:

> Preserve the thought functioning, preserve the creativity and the pleasures that result from them and, often, super invest this pleasure [...]; we know it can preserve friendships and professional relations and only conflict with the beloved relationship, with the one he wanted to love or the one whose love is not according to what he himself defines by this term (1985, p. 161-162).

It is in this conflict that pleasure becomes random or impossible. Due to this impossibility, an aggressiveness part unties from the sexual and looks for his achievements in the external environment, whether through an aggressive behavior towards the other, or through self-aggressiveness. Thus, this aggressiveness emerges from the refusal of the other to the expected pleasure.

Regarding this aggressiveness, Aulagnier adds that "in the neurosis the drive to death can only succeed because 'I' refuses the suffering cause by the absence of a pleasure to which he does not want to renounce, although the eventual realization of such pleasure implies the guilt of having transgressed the incest prohibition" (1985, p. 162). On neurosis, the impulsive implication only becomes possible if Eros, the life drive, finds the objects which can be invested. On the other hand, the aggressive response the neurotic directs to the other or to himself is, ultimately, due to the impossibility of, simultaneously, perform the incest and renounce the incestuous desire, being the guilt a result of this impossibility.

Conclusion

From the literature review, this article brought the neurotic potentiality concept, noting that, although Aulagnier has a clinical experience more aimed at the psychosis field, she also left a legacy to the neurosis field, connecting it to the repressed childhood desires manifestations, being the conflict intensity between 'I' and his Ideals what will define the neurotic conflict. In this field there is a former childish demand of these children desires being aimed at new people, although there is an ignorance of the sexual component neurotic 'I' included in this demand. Therefore, this article is completed highlighting that the neurotic symptomatology will manifest when the neurotic 'I' invests in another 'I' because he wanted to be loved and protected, willing to satisfy his former childish demand, but thanks to the repression effect, this sexual pleasure becomes impossible.

Bibliographical References

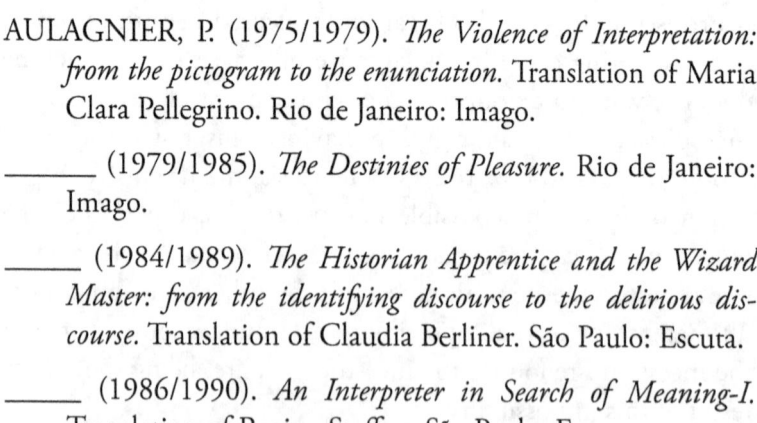

AULAGNIER, P. (1975/1979). *The Violence of Interpretation: from the pictogram to the enunciation.* Translation of Maria Clara Pellegrino. Rio de Janeiro: Imago.

_____ (1979/1985). *The Destinies of Pleasure.* Rio de Janeiro: Imago.

_____ (1984/1989). *The Historian Apprentice and the Wizard Master: from the identifying discourse to the delirious discourse.* Translation of Claudia Berliner. São Paulo: Escuta.

_____ (1986/1990). *An Interpreter in Search of Meaning-I.* Translation of Regina Steffen. São Paulo: Escuta.

The clinical method relevances for the psychotherapy beginning

The clinical method: a brief introduction

In this first part it is necessary to make a brief explanation about what would be the clinical method, bringing some fundamental points of its historical aspects, and emphasizing the clinical observation importance (or not); since the discussion on this is of fundamental importance for the analyst formation.

According to Berlinck (2011), since the Ancient Greeks, man is dedicated to observe things and the other men. However this observation [...] has always been merged with magical and religious imagery. At this time, the nature and subjective concepts still were not developed. For the Greeks there was no difference between nature and culture. With the Renaissance, the so asleep body becomes admired for its aesthetics. It is during Renaissance that several changes occur in the way to think the outside world, allowing a rupture between the observer and the observed.

Berlinck (2011) points out that from the 18th century arises in Europe a movement called naturalism giving scientific status to the nature observation. Both the modern science and the naturalism believe that the outside world can be apprehended and understood from the manifested phenomena observation and classification. Unlike the antique, the observer assumes a neutral character, realizing the outside world through his observation. In addition, modern medicine, such as psychiatry, has its origin in naturalism. This as a move that provided a scientific basis to the nature phenomena observation from the apprehension and understanding of natural manifestations.

In naturalism there is a neutral observer who would be "somebody who is capable of sensibly apprehending the world without interfering in it through visions or prejudices [...]. The clinical method is like this, the way adopted by naturalists for the nature knowledge" (Berlinck, 2011). We can find the clinical method foundation in the observations of several naturalists, especially in Darwin's observations about the evolution of our species. Therefore, thanks to naturalism and the observation of several species made by Darwin, the classification system arises, being the 'uninterested observation' of fundamental importance for the emergence of qualifying systems that are still present in the clinical method.

For Berlinck (2011) the notion of 'uninterested observation' will evolve into what, later, became known as 'evaluative neutrality' that determines, in part, the clinical method. The neutral place, the neutrality, is of fundamental relevance to the clinical method. The neutral seeks to capture the essence of the speech in question, highlighting the observed uniqueness. It is the observer (the analyst) position interaction and the observed (the patient) that produces the subjectivity that determines the observer's thought, highlighting the discourse subjectivity of the clinical case in question.

At the clinic, the neutral is formless and not distributed in any genre, being the unknown always said in the neutral. The neutral clinic is a clinic distant from the medical clinic and the psychological clinic: it is an observation clinic. Many clinicians cannot see the patient in the uniqueness of his symptom, because they are immersed in the theory, but before deepening this discussion (which will be made in the following topic), I would like to stress that the anatomy consolidation had a wide impact on the clinical method and psychiatry.

According to Berlinck (2011), anatomy allowed the medicine to become governed by the normal-pathological conceptual pair determined by the organ injury. The anatomy consolidation focused on internal medicine (the organs injury), determining the normal and pathological concept. So, in this change, the diseases cause must be sought inside the body and no longer on its outside.

At this moment, "the clinic gains its full meaning, leaning on the sick to auscultate, touch, percuss, smell, palpate, observe, but, above all to translate these signs, a true nature language, in visible clippings drown on the body that gets sick" (Berlinck, 2011). The observable and visible gains strength at this time. Everything that is seen must have a correlated knowledge, but not everything that was seen presented a correlated organic; in other words, not every symptom presented an organic cause. Thus, as many symptoms did not present organic causes, it was left to psychiatrists the clinical narrative resource.

At the end of the 19th century, psychiatrist physicians who bended over the mental illness, the famous alienists, were increasingly distancing from the pathological organism, constituting, according to Berlinck (2011), "[…] a rich psychopathology [...]. The classic psychopathology contributed, decisively, to what can be called the 'Freudian revolution' […]".

But after all, what would be then the clinical method? According to Berlinck (2011), the clinical method is far from the clinic. This is a constant and recurring series between clinician and patient. The method can be considered the course of a treatment that occurs at the clinic, being this the construction of events that occurred in this space. The clinician comes to encounter an obscure and dangerous body and this will acquire a form at the time when he starts verbalizing about his suffering. Thus, the body, the symptom, is being revealed to the clinician. That is why the clinical narrative is so critical for who observes this body.

According to Berlinck (2011), the psychopathological narrative is a credible story that builds a shape and a strangely familiar figure without worrying about the sensors inherent to that tradition. In the face of madness, just the more naturalistic possible narrative remains, because it allows the comment aimed at understanding the case. It is in the case narrative where the symptom is, but in the symptom, what is revealed not always is what wants to be revealed. On the other hand, the symptom has caricatured dimension, such as the obsessive ceremonial, since all symptom is revealed in a way that is not harmonious.

At the same time in which the symptom is revealed, it hides other manifestations. The symptom can be considered as everything that is manifested in the clinic, being this a compromise between the unconscious (the displacement) and what is being displaced, repressed. Thus, the clinician (Freudian or not) has to be mindful of what is manifested in the clinic, not forgetting that in the clinical method, the analyst should focus his attention on neutral, being this a space that could be occupied (or not) by this analyst in the future.

If the symptom is what puts himself into the clinic, it is up to the analyst not to forget the symptom bifid nature, not worrying about what is only revealed, since every symptom is obscure in its roots: it has a side that reveals and the other that obscures. The standardized symptom is not only what is repeated, but it is a place of psychic pathos manifestation. This can contain an individual and social, familiar or cultural, singular and collective side of the space occupied by this patient.

The treatment beginning: The initial observations relevance for the clinical method enrichment

The analyzed patient voice, at the treatment beginning, is always mysterious and enigmatic, since these are the ones that reflect his own pathology. These voices raise questions on the analyst himself and are related to impulsive manifestations and the analyzed patient desire.

The patient voice is a desire expression, a cure desire, moved by the life drive. If the cure desire is the desire to eliminate the pain caused by psychic suffering, the clinic, in first instance, aims the life movement.

Freud, in 1913, writes the article *About the Treatment Beginning* in which he emphasizes the fundamental pillars of an analysis beginning. In this text, he points out that "making a mistake [...] is a lot more serious to the psychoanalyst that for the clinician psychiatrist [...] With regard to the psychoanalyst, however, if the case is unfavorable, he made a practical mistake: he was responsible for unnecessary expenses and discredited his treatment method" (1913, p. 140). Remembering that Freud made preliminary diagnoses, because he never treated paraphrenia cases, but only transfer neurosis cases in which hysteria, phobia and obsessional neurosis are comprised.

At the treatment beginning, the first symptoms clinical observations are of fundamental importance for the resistance analysis and, consequently, the transfer, this being considered an ancient imago movement towards the analyst.

For Freud "the first symptoms [...] such as his first resistance, may have special interest and reveal a complex that directs his neurosis. One should wait until the transfer [...] has become a resistance" (1913, p.153-154). It is in the first psychoneurotic symptoms observations that one can notice the resistance serving as a spring, a springboard, for the transfer. It is in this duality (between resistance and transfer) that the narrations from patients become a fertile soil where the identificatory story germinates from each one in its uniqueness, such as its resistance. But how should the analyst proceed at this moment?

It is up to the analyst to give some time for what is in the patient fertile soil spontaneously germinating through his free associations. And for this, it is also up to the analyst to interpret the place which is intended by the patient imagoes, and such imagoes being from his remote childhoods figures. Thus, this place occupied by the neutral, a space that will be occupied by the analyzed transfer, is of paramount importance for the resistance understanding, as well as the symptoms verbalized by the patient.

It is the pace of Priapus[1], of the patient free associations fertility, that this analyst will protect and 'humidify' his patient verbalizations, becoming a projective mirror of this fertile body and favoring that the psychoanalysis fundamental rule – the free association – is manifested.

For this body manifesting, anchored by verbalizations, it is necessary to build a good rapport between the analyst and the analyzed. This means that this trust link between both and from which it will be possible to observe this patient history fertility, being the clinic a place which provides the conditions for this nature to manifest. It is in this nature where the clinical method richness lives, as it is in the patient narrations observation and by its symptomatic manifestations that we can hear the voice that is crying for understanding of his psychic dynamics, regardless of his psychodiagnosis.

In addition to understanding the patient transference phenomena and the free associations, the analyst must also understand his own resistance as a professional, since his own countertransfer can stiffen the analysis progresses.

At the Nuremberg Congress, to point out the psychoan-alytic technique, Freud discusses the countertransfer "as a result of the patient influence about the unconscious feelings [from the analyst]. No psychoanalyst advances beyond what his own complex and internal resistances allow [...]" (1910, p. 150). That is why every analysis progresses through the analyst analy-sis, although the countertransfer, these 'analyst unconscious feel-ings', still provide several discussions in the psychoanalytic field.

---

1 Priapus is the Greek god of fertility, son of Dionysus and Aphrodite.

On the other hand, beyond the contertransfer, it is up to the analyst to rethink his owns formation, since the orthodoxies placed by the psychoanalytic collegiate hinder his ethical and professional growth, and through his rationalizations and intellectualizations, impregnate these patients with diagnoses, labeling them. This means that many of the clinical discussions are aimed at diagnosis and not the clinical observation that each patient, with his uniqueness, can contribute to the technique studies progress in psychoanalysis.

Some schools of psychoanalysis study (such as the Lacanian school) are captured by the joints of its own theory, sustaining themselves on a theoretical rigidity and phallic puerile narcissism in which the links with other schools (such as the Klenian) becomes a source of endless criticism without convincing clinical support.

On the other hand, these schools forget the clinician and the observations richness resulting from its students (or disciples, at worst) clinical practice. These clinical observations are responsible for the psychoanalysis progresses, but such progresses can only occur when there a breach or theoretical orthodoxy, enabling a flexibility in clinical discussions; since when closing in its own orthodoxy, these schools stagnate the clinical discussions, making its future analysts professional growth impossible, and not allowing the observations of each patient uniqueness, regardless of his clinical diagnosis and the school to which his analyst belongs. Therefore, it is up to the analyst leave this pace provided by minority and walk beyond the theoretical identificatory imagoes relevant to his formation, choosing the clinical method that can best guide him.

The clinical method and the analyst formation

In the discussion about this method, we cannot forget that this can be considered a path that is linked to the analyst formation. In this method, the neutral place occupied by the patient is of utmost importance, because this is filled by the voice that calls. A good example is when we receive a patient and this raises several fantasies guided by the psychoanalytic theory to which we are subjected, raising certain questions.

These are the questions that may enrich the clinical practice and the later theoretical discussions, although we cannot deny the voiced complaints. This means that it is in the ruminant thoughts intricacies or on everyday dissatisfaction complaints that we encounter the singular desire of each patient and his symptomatic verbalizations.

Here lies the great danger: The clinician, in his formation and in the search of the analyzed transfer understanding, can support on aggressive interventions to the patient. But when should the clinician start these interventions?

According to Freud "only after an effective transfer is established in the patient, a suitable rapport with him" (1910, p. 152). If the patient arrives at the clinician as someone who has something to reveal, it is in this something to reveal, to hear, that the clinician must observe the transfer phenomenon to start his interventions and understand the patient nature. As the human being has an inner world inhabited by words, he resists in expressing his words, although these are revealed by his symptoms nature.

Remember that the word nature is derived from the Greek *physis* and represents what germinates and has movement. This conception assumes the existence of a real movement, the life drive, such as the clinician expects his patient life movement and associations fertility. This means that the manifestation expected in the clinic is the word linked to the voice, being the body the fertile soil and this voice nature would be manifested. On the other hand, for this voice manifestation it is necessary that a protection exists, being the clinician presence fundamental to ensure fertility, providing the conditions necessary for this nature manifestation.

It is in the patient human nature that his words are manifested, his body movement, and his manner of dressing and to position himself against his internal conflicts. In this nature, the clinician also faces the way this patient feels his smells, the way he relates his fantasies and etc.

The dream may also be considered a manifestation of this voice that echoes in the clinic. While putting his dreams in words, it is up to the analyst to understand the tonality, the intensity of this voice echoed in the analyzed words. Thus, the clinician formation, in general, also implies in listening to the sound of this disharmony or confrontational voice.

These words, sounds, smells, dreams, fantasies, enrich the analyst formation, since he is entitled to observe and listen to these various manifestations. If this comes to listen and observe a single manifestation of this 'voice', both if it comes from his theoretical formation or from a single symptom observed from his patient – and not his libidinal and identificatory history – this clinician is fated to his own alienation.

An example would be the own notes about Freud about the future progress of psychoanalysis. Remember that he never analyzed cases of psychosis, being the Schreber analysis conducted through the analysis of his own autobiographical narrative. For Freud it falls to the future psychoanalysis progresses analyze the psychotic, a fact that occurred with Melanie Klein contributions, from the children's analysis, when she found that her psychotic patients also performed the transfer, a fact that was not recognized by Freud, since, in his understanding, the transfer would not be possible in psychosis.

Conclusion

From the discussions exposed above, we can conclude that the analyst must seek each patient essence, understanding and respecting the therapeutic link. It is up to the analyst to wait the necessary time for what is in the patient soil germinating through his free associations, corporal manifestations, his parapraxis, his verbalizations, etc. Thus the patient would be a fertile soil from the singular nature of his life story, being the clinical practice, a personal analysis (from the analyst) and the supervision of each case (in its particularity) fundamental to the clinician formation.

So that for this singular nature manifestation it is necessary that the analyst can decode the transfer and the resistance of his analyzed, such as his own countertransfer. It is in this movement between the analyzed and towards the analyst that this becomes the receptacle of the infantile imagoes, being the observations resulting from this phenomenon fundamental for his clinical practice enrichment. During this movement, the analyzed voice would represent an impulsive movement, of life and his search for healing.

The clinical method is not an experimental method nor a qualitative method, but a long way to be crossed by the analyst during his clinical practice, since his formation coincides with this practice. Therefore, the clinician formation is linked to the enigmatic character of this voice that resonates and echoes in the clinic, during the clinical care, in which there is an insatiable search to understand it, emerging from this many questions that come to enrich the analyst clinical formation and the contemporary psychoanalysis progress.

Bibliographical References

BERLINCK, M. T. *The clinical method 1*. In: University Association for Research in Fundamental Psychopathology. Available on: http://pt.fundamentalpsychopathology.org Access on: 10/11/2011.

_____. *The clinical method 2*. In: University Association for Research in Fundamental Psychopathology. Available on: http://pt.fundamentalpsychopathology.org Access on: 10/11/2011.

_____. *The clinical method 3*. In: University Association for Research in Fundamental Psychopathology. Available on: http://pt.fundamentalpsychopathology.org Access on: 10/11/2011.

_____. *The clinical method 4*. In: University Association for Research in Fundamental Psychopathology. Available on: http://pt.fundamentalpsychopathology.org Access on: 10/11/2011.

_____. *The clinical method 5*. In: University Association for Research in Fundamental Psychopathology. Available on: http://pt.fundamentalpsychopathology.org Access on: 10/11/2011.

FREUD, S. (1910/1996). *The Future Perspectives of Psychoanalytic Therapy*. *ESB*, vol. XI. Rio de Janeiro: Imago.

_____. (1913/1996). *About the Beginning of the Treatment (New Recommendations About the Psychoanalysis Technique)*. *ESB, vol. XII*. Rio de Janeiro: Imago.

Henrique Scatollin

Psychoanalytic contributions of Karl Abraham to the Freudian legacy

Introduction

This article aims to highlight the German psychoanalyst Karl Abraham contributions to Freudian psychoanalysis. To highlight these contributions, this article makes a brief bibliographical survey on Freudian work, bringing Freud's conceptions about the oral and anal-sadistic stages. Throughout this bibliographic survey, in a second moment, are highlighted the German psychoanalyst Karl Abraham contributions to that libido theory, such contributions that were incorporated into Freudian metapsychology throughout the decade of 30.

For starting this article, we would like to emphasize that, for Freud, in the early psychic constitution, the baby is fitted with an id, and then, of a body ego (derived from the body sensations), targeting the establishment of an ideal ego narcissistically invested by the parents. On the other hand, in the libidinal development level, he claims that during the early years of a child's life there are "organizations of sexual life in the genital areas that have not yet assumed its predominant role" (Freud, 1905). These organizations are defined as pre-genital organizations (such as the oral and anal-sadistic organization) and infant genital (also known as phallic phase).

Freud initially points the anal-sadistic organization, in 1913, when publishing the article *The Disposition to Obsessional Neurosis*, and only in 1915, two years after this publication, he refers to the oral organization, when publishing the edition of the *Three Assays*. Thus, the notion of anal stage appears prior to the oral stage. In both organizations, the compelling are partial and their goals are the satisfaction upon appropriate stimulation of their erogenous zones.

Freud (1905) comprises erogenous zone as "a part of the skin or the mucosa where certain types of stimulation causes pleasurable feelings of certain quality". These dominant erogenous zones are the mouth (in oral phase) and the anus (in anal-sadistic phase); but, in a footnote added to the *Three Assays*, Freud (1905) stresses that "the use of other observations led me to assign the erotogenic property to all parts of the body and all internal organs". Freud, when deepening the discussions on the erogenous zones, understands that any point of the skin or the mucosa can take his burden as an erogenous zone. Such a claim is reiterated at the end of his work when he points out that "the most prominent parts of the body that this libido originates are known by the name of 'erogenous zones', although, in fact, the entire body is an erogenous zone of this type" (Freud, 1940).

The oral phase

The first pre-genital organization is the oral (or cannibalistic). For Freud (1905), in this organization, "the sexual activity has not yet separated from nutrition, nor differentiates opposing currents inside it". In this organization there is already a division between active or passive current. Sexual pleasure is related to buccal excitement and to suction, since at the beginning of the baby's life, the psychic activity focuses on providing oral zone's needs satisfaction, such as suck milk from the mother breast and such another object to replace the mother breast, such as the baby bottle. The act of sucking on the mother breast is the main activity that provides pleasure to the baby, where his lips behave as an erogenous zone. Thus, sexuality begins to manifest itself shortly after the first satisfaction experience, during and after breastfeeding, when the baby starts sucking the mother breast and, later, a pacifier or finger, the latter being an autoerotic child sexual manifestation.

For Freud (1905), "the child act that sucks is determined by the search for a pleasure ever experienced and now remembered". The child, due to his first enjoyable experiences strives to repeat it, since suck breast (or bottle) might provide him pleasure. In this first phase, the oral eroticism is in the foreground and the satisfaction sought through the erogenous zone of the lip when sucking her breast, thumb and pacifier aims to pursuit the previously experienced pleasure. Therefore, the erogenous oral zone persists throughout the individual life, near the erogenization of other body areas. Persisting in the erogenization, these kids, once adults, tend to be appreciative of kissing, drinking and smoking pleasure[2].

According to Freud (1921), in this organization, "the sexual target consists in the incorporation of the object, model that later will play, in the form of an identification, a psychic important role". During the oral phase, the goal is the embodiment and the master relates that this incorporation is the prototype of the first child identifications.

On the *New Conferences*, when addressing the oral phase, Freud (1933) reiterates that "the erogenous zone of the mouth dominates what can be called the sexual activity from this period of life"; but shortly thereafter, declares that "this repetition [of oral phase] was necessary, so that I could use it as a starting point for an account of the progress in our knowledge". This progress in the psychoanalytic knowledge is related to Karl Abraham thesis on pre-genital phases which focuses on the libido development.

Thus, in his contributions to Freudian metapsychology, Abraham (1921) declares:

---

2 Libido fixation points at this stage (and possible libido regressions) may develop symptoms of feeding disorders (such as anorexia and bulimia) in adulthood.

> We are obliged to admit that there is a differentiation within the oral phase of libido [...]. In the primary level of that phase, the child's libido is linked to the sucking act. This act is the incorporation [...]. Still there is no differentiation between the child that sucks and the breast that feeds. Furthermore, the child has no feelings of hate or love. Their mental state is therefore free, at this stage, of all ambivalence manifestations [...]. In the biting stage of the oral phase, the individual incorporates the object in itself and, thus, destroys it [...]. This is the state in which predominate the cannibalistic drives. It is at this stage that the ambivalent attitude of the ego with his/her object begins to develop.

Through his clinical experience with melancholic patients, Abraham proposed to subdivide the oral procedure in two stages: the precocious oral phase (the milk suction phase) and the sadistic-oral phase (of biting). The latter corresponds to the appearance of the teeth. In this, the bite and devour activity implies an object destruction; as the first ambivalent drives towards the embedded object begin to emerge.

Freud (1933) incorporates this subdivision in his psychosexual development theory, postulating:

> We can be proud of having learned a lot of new things, especially about the first libido organizations, and we have gotten a clearer understanding of the importance of what is old; and to demonstrate this I will give you at least some examples. Abraham showed, in 1924, that one can distinguish two stages in the sadistic-anal phase [...]. Similarly we are certain to make a similar subdivision in the first phase, the oral phase. In the first stage [the oral], what is in question is only the oral incorporation, there is absolutely no ambivalence in relation to the object - the mother breast. The second

stage, characterized by the appearance of the bite activity, can be described as 'oral sadistic'. This shows, for the first time, the ambivalence phenomena, which becomes so clear, later, in the anal-sadistic phase.

This subdivision in Freud oral phase is maintained until the end of his work, when he says that "during this phase [...], sporadically already occur sadistic drives, along with the appearance of the teeth" (Freud, 1940). The master is referring to the sadistic drives of biting and devour the object (the mother breast) that appears at the end of the oral phase.

Anal-sadistic phase

The second pre-genital phase described by Freud is the anal-sadistic. In this organization, "the component instincts that dominate this pre-genital organization of sexual life are anal-erotic and the sadistic" (Freud, 1913). In this organization, the active trend (of domain) is powered by the sadism and the passive tendency by the anal eroticism.

According to Freud (19905), at this phase, "the division into opposites that pervades the sexual life is already constituted, but they still cannot be called masculine and feminine, but active and passive". At this stage, the dominant erogenous zone is the anal. The activity is a result of the domination drive (sadism) through the body muscles and the intestine erogenous mucosa becomes the organ of the passive sexual target (of anal eroticism). Concomitantly to the retention or expulsion of the faeces there are partial drives that act in an autoerotic way. So, at this stage, the opposite impulsive pairs are already developed, i.e., the ambivalence between active (sadism) and passive (masochism) is already present.

Freud (1905) emphasizes that the "intestinal catarrhs in the more early childhood leave the child 'nervous' [...]. In the later neurotic illness, they have a determining influence in the somatic manifestation of neurosis". The anal erogenous zone preserves, in adult life, a considerable portion of the genital excitability and, in most remote childhood, certain intestinal disorders may have provoked intense excitations. In these disorders, the boy can come to feel pleasure in erogenous stimulation while retaining the fecal mass. This retention denotes the manifestation of sadistic drives of the child, providing him the (dis)pleasure. The constipation so frequent in childhood provides the anal zone masturbatory stimulation and may be demonstrating the child pertinacity in relation to people who take care of him. And when they grow, this game to retain faeces may be symbolically present in the special scatological rituals, in ceremonial acts and similar acts which are carefully kept confidential by the neurotic individual. Thus, these disturbances have a determining influence on neurosis manifestation in adulthood.

When writing *Character and Anal Eroticism*, Freud (1908) takes the point of view of the children who fell pleasure in feaces retention, postulating: "we deduce from such indications that these people were born with a sexual constitution in which the anal zone erogenous zone is exceptionally strong [...]". In the course of psychic development, the excitements from the anal erogenous zone suffer several variations, and a large part of these excitations can be deflected of sexual purposes and directed towards other purposes, and this process is called sublimation. As a result of the anal eroticism sublimation the triad of three characteristics is formed comprising a series of character traits: the orderly (those who fulfill their duties), parsimonious and obstinate people. Both the order, and the parsimony and obstinacy are interconnected with each other.

In addition, the master states that "the feaces are the child first gift, the first sacrifice in the name of his affection, a part of his body that is ready to share, but only with someone whom he loves" (Freud, 1918). The act of defecating offers the first opportunity for which the child must choose between a narcissistic attitude or an attitude of object love. This means that of he shares his feaces on behalf of his love or retains it with the autoerotic or aggressiveness satisfaction purpose. The child can use the feaces as an expression of defiance, symbolically denoting his hatred; or on the contrary, when ceding the feaces, he is expressing his feelings of love. Thus, the act of giving the faeces to who this child loves is the first moment in which the boy shares a piece of his own body in order to win the favors of anybody else and this act symbolizes, primarily, the narcissistic love transition (if he retained the faeces) for the object love.

In addition to the anal eroticism fortification that can leave a great inclination to homosexuality, Freud (1933) states that the 'old interest for the feaces becomes the great value granted to gold and money [...]". The interest for the money is taken from the anal-erotic sources, since the commitment on defecation disappears in later stages of adulthood, becoming the value granted to gold and money. Thus, the interest for the money enables the transfer of early drive to this new object.

In his contributions to anal-sadistic phase, the German physician and psychoanalyst Karl Abraham (1921) says:

> The psychoanalytic experience has forced us to state the existence of a pre-genital phase of libidinal development [anal phase] and we are currently taken to assume that this phase contains, in itself, two different levels. In the subsequent level, conservative trends prevail to retain and control the object, whereas in the older level, the hostile trends to the object – to destroy it and lose it – come to the foreground [...]. This differentiation of the sadistic-anal phase in a primitive stage and another posterior appears to have a radical importance because

the dividing line between these two phases provides a decisive change in the individual attitude towards the outside world.

In the *New Conferences*, Freud (1933) incorporates this contribution of Abraham to his theory, as he says: "we can be proud of having learned a lot of new things, especially about the first libido organizations [...]. Abraham showed, in 1924, that one can distinguish two stages in the sadistic-anal phase". The master is referring to the subdivision of anal-sadistic phase. The first of these stages is dominated by trends of destroying and losing, and the second stage by affectionate tends towards the objects (like the trends to maintain and possess)[3].

According to Freud (1940), the amplitude of sadistic drives "is much higher in the second phase [anal-sadistic] for being the so sought satisfaction in aggression and in the excretory function". In this stage, the sadism comprises the drive fusion of purely libidinal drives (of Eros) and destructive (of Thanatos); but the master relates that "it would be a mistake to assume that these three phases [oral, anal and phallic] succeed clearly. One may appear in addition to another; they may overlap and may be present side by side" (Freud, 1940). The predominance of one phase in relation to another does not occur so suddenly and so gradually. At the end of the oral phase the early sadistic drives emerge during the appearance of teeth. The baby can come to experience pleasure, in a sadistic way, when trying to suck the milk. These sadistic drives become common in anal-sadistic phase and for being the satisfaction sought in aggression and in the excretory function. On the other hand, it is desirable to emphasize that throughout these phases (the oral and the anal-sadistic) some development inhibitions may occur lead-

---

3 Let us remember that Abraham assigns this second tendency to obsessive neurosis and the first to melancholy.

ing to libido fixations. Consequently, future libido regressions during adult genital phase can cause certain psychopathologies, such as obsessional neurosis (which features a fixation on the anal-sadistic phase).

Final Considerations

The study of the oral and anal-sadistic phases divisions proposed by Abraham is of paramount importance for the differential diagnosis in the clinical context, as it allows a differentiation in understanding the psychic dynamics of a melancholic patient from an obsessive one.

In proposing this subdivision, this German psychoanalyst associates ambivalent drives already present at the end of oral phase with the aggressive drives, of attack to mother breast. In addition to these contributions to the oral phase, he also highlights the anal expulsive phase interconnecting it with melancholic destructive movements, of object annihilation. And when emphasizes the anal-retentive phase (present at the end of anal-sadistic organization), Abraham associates this with the retentive movement of object control. Therefore, the dynamics of symbolically retaining and expelling feaces can be considered a dividing line between the melancholy, in which there are movements of destruction of the identified object, and the obsessional neurosis, in which there are control movements of the beloved object.

On the other hand, these contributions from Abraham to Freudian psychoanalysis came to influence the Klenian theory of object relations, in which the British psychoanalyst has preserved this concept, using it to develop his metapsychology on the positions theory, such as his conception of envy.

Bibliographical References

ABRAHAM, K. (1921/1970). *Psychoanalytic Theory of Libido.* Translation of Christiano Monteiro Oiticica. 6th edition. Rio de Janeiro: Imago.

FREUD, S. (1905/1996). *Three Essays On the Sexuality Theory. ESB*, vol. VII Rio de Janeiro: Imago.

_____. (1908/1996). *Character and Anal Eroticism. ESB*, vol. IX, Rio de Janeiro: Imago.

_____ (1909/1996). *Notes On a Case of Obsessional Neurosis. ESB*, vol. X, Rio de Janeiro: Imago.

_____. (1913/1996). *The Inclination to Obsessional Neurosis – A Contribution to the Problem of Neurosis.ESB*, vol. XII, Rio de Janeiro: Imago.

_____.(1918/1996). *History of an Infantile Neurosis.ESB*, vol. XVII, Rio de Janeiro: Imago.

_____. (1921/1996). *Group Psychology and the Ego Analysis. ESB*, vol. XVIII, Rio de Janeiro: Imago.

_____. (1923/1996). *The Ego and the Id.* ESB, vol. XIX, Rio de Janeiro: Imago.

_____. (1933/1996). *Conference XXXI – The Dissection of Psychic Personality. ESB*, vol. XXII. Rio de Janeiro: Imago.

_____. (1933/1996).*Conference XXXII – Anxiety and Instinctive Life.ESB*, vol. XXII, Rio de Janeiro: Imago.

_____. (1940/1996). *Psychoanalysis Outline. ESB*, vol. XXIII, Rio de Janeiro: Imago.

MASSON, Jeffrey M. (1986). *The complete correspondence of Sigmund Freud to Wilhelm Fliess 1887-1904.* Rio de Janeiro: Imago.

Doubt and guilty: A theoretical and clinical study on the identificatory problem in an obsessional neurosis case

Introduction

The construction of this thesis, which is still in progress, consists of a theoretical and clinical study on the identificatory problem in obsessional neurosis. For this purpose, it resorts the guilty unconscious feeling and the doubt of an obsessive patient, unveiling them as an anchor point for this problem understanding.

The present study about this problem is the result of my clinical observations of patients who I consider obsessive neurotic. During these patients psychotherapeutic treatment, it was noticed that the identificatory problem understanding was of fundamental importance for the understanding of the unconscious feeling of guilty, since it highlighted the symbolic 'debt' with the father. This means that this identification revealed the ambivalence in the father-son relationship, which is fundamental in understanding this neurosis and its symptoms.

It is highlighted that this idea of 'symbolic debt' comes from my singular reading of the text *Debt and Guilty*, of Contardo Calligaris, in which the author states that, in the relationship of the obsessive with his father, "it means to create an inspector, more specifically to call a creditor to verify that the debt is being paid (the study is due to the father, and receive a carnal tribute to his superiority" (1991, p.21). Due to the existence of a hard superego, that comes as an inspector, I note that many obsessive patients nourish a relationship of ambivalence regarding the father, and this is made explicit in his obsessive symptoms, such as in doubts and in certain obsessive rituals. I highlight that, in certain cases, this ambivalence relationship is directly linked to the identification with the father, being the (un)conscious guilty feeling a result of this identificatory problem.

In addition, the interest in the study of this identificatory problem in obsessional neurosis is present since the time I finished my master's degree, in 2007, when I defended the dissertation entitled *A Theoretical Clinical Study on the Ceremonial Act in Obsessional Neurosis*. In this research, I emphasized that the ritual to hide knives represented for the psychic constitution of an obsessive patient. During the ritual, this patient great fear (or desire) was being anally penetrated by knives. Thus, this clinical case analysis, which I named *The Knives Man*, opened the first doors for future questions on this issue, being the understanding of Bleichmar (1993) on the incorporation of paternal phantasmagorical sadistic penis of paramount importance to understand the father-son identificatory relationship and the homosexuality ghosts, such as passivity, that open from this anal incorporation.

So, this indication of Bleichmar (1993) also made me wonder about Paulo identificatory problem, arousing me to a reflection on this subject. This means that in my clinic listening and, from the patient associations, I noticed that the presence of a paternal identification made it possible to understand how the doubt symptom and the guilty unconscious feeling were put to Paulo. And, in my clinical experience with Paulo and other obsessive patients, I understand that the passivity ghosts (from the father's penis anal incorporation)become strengthened by the libidinal regression to the sadistic-anal phase, delighting all the obsessive identificatory problem through doubts (in which we find the ambivalent drives to the parents), and guilty, in which the incestuous desire regarding the mother and the aggressive drives toward the father pay the due price.

Thus, this work aims to focus on the relevance of the

identificatory problem for understanding the guilty unconscious feeling and the doubt in this neurosis. For this study, I chose a patient who I believe is obsessive neurotic, and whose understanding of a possible libidinal and identificatory story denotes this ambivalence relation towards the father. This patient, who I identify with the fictitious name of Paulo, seeks psychotherapy due to the ruminant thoughts of his father death (and his father had died two years ago), and also complained a lot of chest pains.

For this case presentation, I will emphasize the therapeutic process occurred since the patient Paulo arrival until his fourth year of psychotherapy. I highlight that in this cutting I find sufficient data for the development of this thesis proposal, i.e., the careful study of the identificatory problem is the guiding axis for understanding the guilty and doubt in the obsessional neurosis cases.

Therefore, for this study, I will be supported by the possible libidinal and identificatory story of patient Paulo, pointing out though his stories, dreams and dissimulating memories, how this problem is manifested in his doubts and his guilty feeling.

Methodology

This study on the identificatory problem in obsessional neurosis is based on psychoanalysis as a theory, therapeutic technique and investigation method of the unconscious. In this study, the texts written by Sigmund Freud on the obsessional neurosis occupy a key position. To these I add the theoretical contributions of Piera Aulagnier for the Freudian metapsychology and psychopathology, since I believe that these provide and understanding of the identificatory problem in this neurosis. Despite this psychoanalyst has not addressed specifically the obsessional neurosis, there are fundamental concepts of her theory that enrich the understanding of the psychic constitution of this research subject.

As I understand the analytical process as "something that you live every day, session after session [...]"(Pontalis, 2002), the annotations from this case occurred shortly after the session ending, respecting the uniqueness and the free associations of this patient.

According to Mezan (1993), "the psychoanalytic literature contains numerous examples and elaborations that serve as a working too [...].These are schemas to correlate data, to infer hypothesis, to suggest derivations". I highlight that my working tools are based on my psychoanalytic reading of Freudian work, the Piera Aulagnier contributions to it, as well as the postulates of Andre Green and Bleichmar on the obsessional neurosis. Thus, it was possible to develop a sustenance building that provided me the support for the study of this problem, enabling the development of the floating theorizing of this clinical case.

These theorizing based on psychoanalytic theory and technique, since this research is of qualitative character and is based on the data analysis of the libidinal and identificatory story of only one patient. This research field had as object Paulo psychic reality and all manifestations of his unconscious. The method used was the data interpretation from their free associations, but also the possibility conditions for the empirical emergence of his unconscious formation.

Results and Discussion

Listening to the reports of death thoughts of this patient, I realized that, in these, the identification with the father revealed a lack, a guilty, in which his ideals were never achieved. It was "in this lack" that, on one hand it was a son complaining about a (dis)pleasure of his symptoms and, on the other, a father that, although dead, reigned in the imagination as if he were still alive, permeating this patient dreams and symptoms. Consequently, Paulo guilty charged its price for the debt with the father, making the doubt a symptomatic manifestation of his ambivalent drives.

On the other hand, in the study of this problem, Paulo's mother had a key role. During the psychotherapeutic process, this became almost "untouchable" in his verbalizations, but over his stories, the 'father' was giving way to the mother. So, the way the mother recognizes the paternal function, the father law, and how it was passed on to the son is a priceless wealth in this case analysis. This means that, for a better understanding of Paulo identificatory problem the presence of this mother is also of extreme importance. And, from the reports of dreams in which the mother figure was present, I developed certain "floating theorizing" (Aulagnier, 1989), which allowed me to suppose how this mother recognizes the paternal function and how the presence of this 'rude' father interdicted Paulo infant desires, leading him to pay a high price for wanting what could not have been desired: the incest and the patricide.

And for deepening on this theory postulate, I would like to come back to the four guiding axis of this problematic, intertwining them with Paulo clinical data, as well as other cases of obsessional neurosis already serviced by me.

The first axes for this problem understanding is supported on the Oedipal resolution of these patients' parents, and which in this study refers, specifically, to the case of Paulo. For this purpose, I resort to the concept of spoken-shadow, since this is directed to the maternal repressed and the spokeswoman notion.

For Aulagnier these relations analysis [spokeswoman, infant body, and the repressing action] will allow the elucidation of this identificatory problem, which has the axis of transmission, subject to subject, of a repressed necessary to the structural requirements of Myself" (1975, p.60). In the case of Paulo, as well as other obsessive patients, the maternal repressed guarded an enormous wealth, since in this it was possible to detect the recognition of a third representative that would mediate the law between the child and the maternal relationship.

This is the paternal function, the father law, already present, since always, in the repressed of Angela and this acknowledged in her husband Claudio the only representative that could legitimize and transmit this law to Paulo. Remember that when making allusion to Paulo father presence in his cemetery dream, this mother pointed out the presence of a third reference. So, Angela recognized in Claudio the paternal function that once her own father passed on her remote childhood. I remember here an old statement by Claudio that symbolically is directed to the parents' desire for this son: his father, in his birth, had to choose between the mother and his life. The answer was clear: the father wanted the two alive of nothing. So, the father wish, the paternal function, was present, since always, side by side with the desire and the maternal function, libidinally investing the small Paulo and enabling the first incorporations that nurtured his identifications since the early childhood.

At this point, the reader might be wondering how this repressed can be transmitted to the obsessive patient. Here I would like to bring a second axis of identificatory problem: the superego identification in obsessions, postulated by Green, in his article *Obsessional Neurosis Metapsychology*, in 1967. I believe that it is through this identification that the maternal and paternal repressed, the moral values and judgments are transmitted from generation to generation, providing a fresh look to the guilty.

For starting this discussion, first, I would like to use the *New Introductory Lectures on Psychoanalysis*, when Freud (1933/1996) says that the superego installation can be classified as a successful example of the parental instance identification, since a child superego does not follow her parents' model, but her parents' superego, enabling the values transmission between the generations. In this clinical case, I suppose that in this process the guilty covers its price for the small Paulo. When internalizing the parents' values in his superego, the father debt, permeated by the unconscious guilty, already finds its origin in the story of Claudio with the father, which name was never mentioned, as well as in the story of Paulo with the father Claudio. Here opens a dubious dilemma: both in his story and in the story of the father, through the identifications, the guilty charges its price. In other words, there is identification to the father, which myth permeates the two generations in this family: the myth of the 'died' father, who still reigns very much alive in this patient family imagination, permeating, also, his funeral rituals.

In addition, it was noticed that his hard superego identification was driving his moral judgments, so striking in his story, as well as in his father Claudio story. And by denying that he did not want to be like his father, Paulo reassumed the identificatory position with him, repeating many demanding behaviors that his own father had in his childhood, although with more controlling contours due to his infantile sadism sublimations.

Still in this second axis, something caught my attention for the understanding of his guilties and uncertainties. If the superego identification reports him to previous generation, feeding his guilty, I find a quote in Green that launches a new understanding on the uncertainty manifestation, when he says: "the doubt towards the father, the obsessive reiterates it expecting to annul it, borrowing from the father's father, to whom the latter remains debtor" (2005, p.227). So, when resorting to the grandfather, whose name was never mentioned, Paulo tries to deceive the movement of his own desire, once that, while staying on the prowl of his fantasies, he waits to delete any trace of a debt that one day he contracted from his own father Claudio, allowing, in his imagination, a free way for the enjoyment of a desired object, but that, due to the presence of this hard superego identification, was never consummated. And here opens the thresholds of his defense mechanisms, providing high doses of (dis)pleasure to his ego, that confronting with his overwhelming superego, develops an unconscious guilty that paralyzed him so much due to his destructive drives.

At this point, I would like to turn to the third axis of the identificatory problem proposed by this thesis: Paulo libidinal and identificatory story, because a brief resumption of this throws new looks for the ambivalence that guided this patient uncertainties in the clinical setting.

In order to accomplish this articulation, I would like to remind that the "I", throughout the story, was constructed through indentificatory dialectic. In this dialectic we find the "three successive times, represented by primary identification [...], specular identification [...]and project identification" (Aulagnier, 1968). Paulo ambivalence, present behind his doubts, resplended the remnants of the demand object relations, present in his pre-genital identification. Currently, the old faeces sacrifice gives room for other ambivalent manifestations; such as avarice, denoting other outlines of his ambivalent movements that are behind his libidinal and identificatory story.

If, at the end of the oral phase, both the father and the mother already moved his ambivalences (remember the primary scene and the speculate identification, such active (sadistic) and passive movements (coming from his anal eroticism) are intensified in the sadistic-anal phase, determining the ambivalence in relation to the male and female representatives in his adult genital organization. And through his manifestations of time and people control, I believe that the sadistic movement has overlapped to the anal eroticism in his remote childhood, with this latter related to the passivity and the masochism that really paralyzed him, holding, partially, his uncertainties and guilties in his adulthood. Thus, both the passivity and the masochism had its roots in Paulo's old anal eroticism, making the anal constipation and his constipations a slight hysterical trait of his symptomatic manifestation.

And from the understanding of this libidinal and identificatory story, I would like to turn to this thesis fourth and final pillar (or axis):the incorporation of the paternal sadistic penis, proposed by Bleichmar (1993). I would like to remember the trunk in the cemetery dream: when being crossed, cornered, by the paternal sadistic penis, Paulo woke up 'distressed', with constipated intestines and ran to the bathroom to 'relieve' the 'constipated' anger to the father, since this castration agent represented the cut in the relationship with his mother. So, in order to internalize this penis, Paulo anally introjected the aggressiveness and the hate projected to Claudio, and this displeasure reported in the dream refers, in my understanding, to the old pleasure of this incorporation, which founded the passive movements of his anal eroticism, feeding the old homosexual desire and, strengthening, with this incorporation, the sadistic aspects of his superego.

This means that, in this psychic instance, this inspector mentioned by Calligaris (1991), are present in the sadistic drives towards the father's body (remember the primary scene of trucks), which were anally incorporated with this paternal attribute, allowing the male sexual identification to Claudio. In addition, in the remnants of this incorporation that are presents in the passivity ghosts that still persisted behind his masochism and his unconscious feeling of guilty, creating obstacles to his cure and encouraging his therapeutic setting resistance.

There is still something in the cemetery dream that needs to be explained. When reporting the dream in which he looked at the mother and she directed her look to the father, appearing the trunk that, in his association, would be the cemetery tree, I understood that on incorporation of this sadistic penis rested the beginning of his guilty, because by incorporating his father law, the incestuous desire would pay its price.

Here was the dilemma of this patient: every time when his identification anxiety (or castration) arose in the setting, he needed to resume the former identificatory position towards Claudio, taking, symbolically, the stick and going fishing. At this moment, as I was saying, it was God and him in this fact, in my understanding it promoted his guilty. And in this guilty intricacies, his ambivalences are intensified, because, once the penis is incorporated, it caused him, symbolically, a coming and going of his obsessive thoughts, such as the old anal penis in the middle of his intestine, providing a masturbatory pleasure in view of his uncertainties.

And for a better understanding of how this incorporation of paternal attribute reflects in this patient identificatory problem, I would like to mention, briefly, the three times of Oedipus proposed by Lacan.

According to this psychoanalyst, in the first time, there is "the relation of the child [...]with the mother desire" (1957-1958, p.208). At this point, Paulo held a privileged place as being the maternal phallus, denoting a merger to maternal omnipotence.

In the second time we have "the moment when the father is felt as the prohibitory. He appears in the mother speech" (1957-1958, p.209). If, at first, Angela maternal speech was captured in a raw state, at this second time, the father's speech appears mediated, but not fully unveiled in Angela maternal speech. We should also remember his gaze pointing to a third reference in the cemetery, and when little Paul turns, symbolically, he faces Claudio.

This oneiric memory can be correlated to the third moment of his Oedipus complex, in which "the father enters the game [...]as the one who has it. He intervenes at this level to provide what is at the cause of the phallic deprivation. It appears, effectively, in the donation act" (Lacan, 1957-1958), namely the phallus donation, law representative, so present in Paulo moralistic speech.

In my understanding, from this third time lies Paulo obsessive problem. When moving from the position of being the maternal phallus to the position of having his father phallus incorporated, through the trunk that cornered him, Paulo incorporates the moral laws and judgments of his micro social environment. These values will guide his ideal ego judgments, feeding, in the future, his guilties.

Therefore, the sadistic penis incorporation opens the intricacies of this patient identificatory problem, positioning in front of this castration problem, since that having the phallus means the possibility of losing it. This fact drives the decline of his Oedipus complex, leading him to identify his heir: and his hard, sadistic and moralist superego. This superego identification in Aulagnier understanding corresponds to the symbolic identification, culminating in the identification to Paulo identificatory project. For this reason he always demanded to be the best father, the best seller, and the best friend.

And as the identificatory project corresponds to the ego ideal in the Freudian theory, I understand that when Green refers to the superego identification as an obsessive problem, I believe that this problem would correspond to the symbolic identification that would culminate with the intensification of internal demands present in the identificatory projects of my obsessive patients, denoting a conflict between Me and my ideals and ensuring, thus, a demanding content meant for themselves. So, this symbolic identification understanding, proposed by Aulagnier, reinforces the assumption proposed by Green for understanding this issue in obsessions.

Before finalizing this article, I would like to elucidate one last issue. Many might be wondering if there is an order of these four axes for the elucidation of an obsessive problem. I highlight that these four axis proposed for the obsessive problem elucidation are interchangeable, i.e., there is no correct sequence or an hierarchy, but no axis can be ignored, since all four are of extreme relevance to the understanding of this obsessive problem, guiding the clinical look of the future analyst when this comes across an obsession case in his office.

Conclusion

My clinical experience with Paulo and other obsessive patients, as well as the principles of Freud (about obsessional neurosis), of Aulagnier (regarding the identificatory dialect in I constitution), of Bleichmar (in relation to the incorporation of the father penis ghost), of Calligaris (which intertwines the doubt and the guilty in relation to the debt that the obsessive nourished towards the father), and of Green (in which he highlights the superego identification) allow me to propose that only by means of a detailed analysis of the identificatory problem, which occurs since the childhood (and the ambivalent relations in the sadistic-anal phase), is when we can understand how each obsessive patient feels regarding the guilty and 'debt' with the father figure, because I consider the debt, the guilty and, consequently, the symbolic debt with the father, the structural engine of this psychopathology.

Therefore, this article postulates that the identificatory problem is the guiding axis for the understanding of the unconscious guilty and the doubt feelings in the obsessional neurosis. For this purpose, four fundamental points are highlighted in understanding this problem: the Oedipal father and mother resolution of each obsessive patient (here including the maternal repressed transmission), the libidinal and identificatory story understanding for these patients "I" constitution, the anal incorporation of paternal sadistic penis (being the ghosts from this incorporation reinforced by the sadistic-anal regression) and the identificatory process with the father figure since the beginning of psychic constitution (culminating with the superego identification). These four points are of extreme importance for the understanding of this problem that underlies the doubt and guilty symptoms, guiding the obsessive patients' analysis and the study problem proposed in this research.

Bibliographical Reference.

AULAGNIER, P.(1975). *The Violence of Interpretation – from pictogram to the enunciation.* Rio de Janeiro: Imago.

BLEICHMAR, S.(1993). *On the Origins of Psychic Subject: from myth to history.* Translation of Kenia M. B. Behr. Porto Alegre: Artes Médicas.

CALLIGARIS, C. (1991). Doubt and Guilt. In: *The Cure.* Psychoanalytic Association of Porto Alegre, nº 5.

FREUD, S. (1933/1996). *New Introductory Conferences on Psychoanalysis.* Rio de Janeiro: Imago.

GREEN, A. (1967/2005). Metapsychology of Obsessional Neurosis. In: *Obsessional Neurosis.* Manoel Tosta Berlinck (org). São Paulo: Escuta.

LACAN, J. (1957-1958/1999). *The Seminar 05: The Formations of the Unconscious.* Translation of Vera Ribeiro. Rio de Janeiro: Jorge Zahar.

MEZAN, R. (1993). What does "research" mean in psychoanalysis? In: SILVA, Maria Emília Lino da (coord). *Research and Psychoanalysis.* Campinas: Papirus.

The Rats Man case and his heritage for the obsessional neurosis study

Introduction

This article aims to perform a historical survey in the Rats Man case, bringing its contributions to the obsessional neurosis study.

Freud began Ernst Lanzer treatment, the Rats Man, on October 1, 1907. This lasted almost one year and was published in 1909. According to Freud, "this case, judged by its extension, for the damages of its consequences, and the own patient's point of view [...], deserves to be classified as a relatively serious case" (1909, p. 139). This means that it was considered a clinical case of chronic obsessional neurosis, which succeeded with the analysis due to the fact that the patient had recovered well. Thus, the treatment led to the patient's personality complete restoration, as well as the extinction of his inhibitions. According to Jones, after the analysis with Freud, "[...] the patient was very successful in life and at work" (1989, p. 267).

In the introductory note to this clinical case, Freud points out:

> "I must confess that I have not managed to penetrate the complicate texture of a case of obsessional neurosis [...]. It must be admitted that an obsessional neurosis is not, in itself, something easy to understand – and much less easy than a case of hysteria [...] The language of an obsessional neurosis [...] is assumed to be only a dialect of hysteria" (1909, p. 140).

It is necessary to emphasize that after leaving the traumatic theory of neuroses in 1897, Freud retakes the study on obsessional neuroses in 1907, in *Obsessive Acts and Religious Practices*. He writes this article in February 1907; but he would have the first contact with the Rats Man only on October 1 of the same year.

In his understanding of this clinical case context, Roudinesco (1998) points out that this was "the second major psychoanalytic treatment conducted by Sigmund Freud, after Dora (Ida Bauer) and before the Wolf Man (Serguei C. Pankejeff). The story of the Rats Man is, without a doubt, the most elaborated, the most structured and the most rigorously logic" (p. 463).

A bit about the Rats Man history

Born in Vienna, in a bourgeois Jewish family, Lanzer was the fourth child of a family with seven children. His father initially loved a poor woman, but then married with the rich Rosa Saborsky, future mother of Lanzer.

The true identity of the Rats Man only became public with the publishing of the book "*Freud and the Rats Man*", written and produced by Patrick Mahony. In this book, he points out that "Freud's publishing did not reveal the real name of his patient, which now can come to the public for the first time – Dr. Ernst Lanzer. This Viennese citizen began his life in January 22, 1878, in a house where there were already three children. Three others still would come [...]" (1991, p.20). Lanzer was born in a middle class family. His parents enjoyed a notoriously happy marriage life. Although his mother Rosa was born in a poor family, she was adopted by her distant cousins, the wealthy Saborskys who raised her here in a severe form. While his father Heinrich, also born in a family of limited resources, came to marry Rosa, the Rats Man mother, who had a standard of living much better than his.

The Rats Man father "was generous by nature, even to the point of secretly paying the rent of his first guest" (Mahony, 1991, p. 21). To the grown children he admitted his failures and bad luck in life. Heinrich, according to Mahony (1991), importuned his wife due to the habits of expelling gases and using expressions such as "anus" and "shit". He reacted to the tricks of his children with severe punishments. Remembering that, in his remote childhood, when being beaten by his father, the Rats Man violently uttered the insult 'you lamp! You towel! You plate!' Shaken by the verbal fury of his son, Heinrich stopped beating him and exclaimed that his son would become a great man or a criminal. Thus, in the Rats Man family it was the abundant verbalization of exclamatory type was very common. The good-humored conversation of the Rats Man also contributed to the lively family atmosphere.

According to Mahony (1991), regarding the Rats Man mother, there is "very little information about her, requiring a restraint use" (p. 23). In the episodes that dealt with the faeces in his childhood, Lanzer was happy, in certain occasions, in being a 'dirty pig'; since he asked his mother to wash his 'anus' only for her saving him from his furious father.

Ernst Lanzer was a religious devotee until his adolescence, period in which he was constantly disturbed by an older friend who sought his friendship solely with the purpose of having access to his house with the goal of flirting one of his sisters, in an affront to the moral sensibilities of this patient.

In 1897, at the age of eighteen, he began his law studies. Soon he fell in love with a little wealthy cousin called Gisela Adler, who he began courting against the wishes of his father, who would prefer a rich woman for his son. After his father's death in 1898, Ernst, like his father, embraced the military career, joining the third Tyrolean Sharpshooters Regiment of the imperial army.

It was in 1901 when he began to be dominated by strange sexual and morbid obsessions. These obsessions initiated concomitantly to the condolences visit to his uncle for the death of his aunt. It is interesting to mention that he manifested a special taste for funerals and rites of death. Due to this taste he received the nickname of 'vulture' by the habit to go to funerals and express sympathy to the desolated relatives. Also in the same time he had acquired the habit of looking at his penis in a mirror to make sure of its erection degree and he had numerous suicide temptations, based on censorship and accusations directed to him. Sometimes he wanted to cut his throat, sometimes he wanted to drown.

In 1902, at the end of his eighth and final semester of law, he cannot even think of rest, because he had to prepare for the third test of the State that would qualify him as a civil servant. At this time he developed a most unusual ritual. Between midnight and one in the morning, he took a break in his studies, opened the front door to the ghost of his father, went back inside, lighted all lights, undressed and looked at his own penis in the mirror to ensure some erection degree. According to Mahony (1991) "[...] sometimes he put another mirror between his legs [...]" (p. 26).

The summer of 1903 was marked by several compulsions; such as cutting his own throat, jumping off a cliff, and running, without rest, under the strong sunlight. He wondered what he could do for his father and he thought to throw into the river, so that no evil could reach his dead father.

According to Mahony (1991) "the following years witnessed a considerable decrease in the pace of Ernst studies, his promotion to reserve Lieutenant, his first sexual intercourse at the age of twenty-six, the plan of his mother for him to marry another woman, and two isolated jobs [...]" (p. 28). Before seeking Freud, he went to Munich to undergo hydrotherapy and at this time he kept permanent sex relations with a waitress.

In 1907, Lanzer conquered his dreamed doctor's degree. In the summer of the same year he took part of military maneuvers in Galicia. During a break, he lost his pince-nez (a small glass) and not willing to delay the departure, he left this fact "aside"; but he telegraphed to the optician for sending him a pair for the next post. During this stop, he sat between two officers, being one of them a Czech captain for which Lanzer had an immense terror; since this captain liked cruelty; as corporal punishment. It was at this time that this captain told him about the rats' punishment.

Then, it was in the summer of 1907 that he heard the cruel captain Nemeczeck, adherent of corporal punishments, telling the story of the oriental torture which consisted in forcing the prisoner to undress and kneel on the floor with the back curved front. In the man's buttocks it was fixed then, by means of a belt, a large perforated bowl where a rat was wide awake. Deprived of food and provoked by a piece of red-iron inserted into a hole in the bowl, the animal tried to escape from the burning and penetrated into the rectum of the begged, inflicting him to bloody wounds. After more or less half an hour, the rat would die and also the prisoner.

Two days later, Lanzer received the pince-nez through the same captain who had told him the torture technique and who informed him that the postal charges should be refunded to the Lieutenant A, official at the post office. At this moment, appeared the sanction in his mind that he should not refund the cash payment or the rat fantasy would materialize regarding his father and the lady.

This means that the means that were related to the payment of this debt included an absurd move to pay the amount to captain A. At this point, the patient thought that if he returned the amount to captain A, the torture would be applied to his loved ones and to combat this thought, he promised to return the amount at any cost. However, when he found the captain A, this secured that he had not paid anything in place of the patient, which set off a great affliction and a complicated plan for the money return.

Thus, Lanzer then had ruminant thoughts around the subject of this debt payment. The story of the rat torture mixed up with the debt and raised in the Rats Man memory another episode involving money. One day, his father had contracted a game debt: he was saved from disgrace by a friend who had lent him the amount required for the payment. His father, at the end of the military service, could not pay this debt to this friend.

Beginning of the Treatment

According to Freud "a young lord or university education introduced himself to me with the assertion that he had always suffered from obsessions, since childhood, but with special intensity in the last four years. The main aspects of his disturbance were fears that something might happen to two people of whom he was very found: his father and a lady that he admired" (1909, p. 143). When looking for Freud, Ernst Lanzer was aware of compulsive drives, such as, for example, an drive of cutting his throat with a razor; subsequently, he created bans, sometimes, in connection with things somewhat unimportant.

According to Roudinesco (1998) "it was this man, obsessed by rats and a debt, who entered the office of Dr. Freud on October 1, 1907. He immediately entered in the game of the free association and he spontaneously began to evoke sexual memories that remounted his age of six" (p. 464). Lanzer has a fear that the rats torture could happen to the woman he loved and his father, even this having died years before. And given the peculiar symptom of fear of rats, this patient became known as the Rats Man.

Throughout the analysis, Freud (1909) was bringing some data relevant to the understanding of this patient's obsessional neurosis.

The father of psychoanalysis highlights that the Rats Man sexual life had been blocked and the masturbation only played a small role on it, when he was 16 or 17 years old. When he was between four and six years of age he intimately touched two nannies who worked at his house, and he constantly had the desire to see naked women. He told Freud that when his governess Fraulein Peter was lying beside him, he crawled under her skirt and touched with the fingers her genitals, getting a burning and tormented curiosity to see the female body. When Lanzer climbed on her bed, he was forced to uncover and touch her, since she had no objections.

At the age of six, he already had erections. He already had the morbid idea that his parents knew his thoughts; explaining this obsession supposing that he revealed his thoughts aloud to his parents, without having listened to it. Thus, he considered that his illness had begun at the age of six.

At this time, when he felt desires related to female nudity, he believed that something bad was going to happen, then he should do anything to avoid them. This something bad would be the death of this father who occupied his mind since childhood.

For Freud (1909), at the age of six, Lanzer already featured an obsessional neurosis, not missing any essential element. Parallel to the obsessive desire, there was an obsessive fear. For Freud (1909), these drives were developed in the prohibition measures that the patient adopted. Therefore, to the father of psychoanalysis, the obsessional neurosis makes it obvious that the factors that will form a psychoneurosis may be found in the patient childhood sexual life and not in his adult life.

The great obsessive fear

When reporting the rats' torture to Freud, Lanzer arose from the couch and asked Freud to spare him from the details explanation. For Freud (1909), at this point, the overcoming of resistances was an act of the treatment, and in anyway, one could be dismissed from it.

When reporting this obsessive fear, Freud (1909) highlights an observation of this patient reporting the rats torture; because at every moment of the story, Freud observed in his face a complex and bizarre expression, an expression that the master understood as a horror to a thrill that even Lanzer ignored.

The fear that his father could die appeared early on the patient's life, to which Freud presented him the idea that behind this fear there would be a desire and a lot of ambivalence in his obsessive symptoms.

According to Freud (1909), in the compulsions to protect someone can be the counterpart of an unconscious desire of destruction. In Lanzer also appeared suicidal desires, for example, like when the patient, missing his beloved, had the drive to cut his own throat. When he already was with the blade in his hands, he thought that it was not so simple and that he should kill the 'old'; that is the grandmother of his girlfriend Gisela; since his beloved was taking care of her sick grandmother. In this case, Freud (1909) said that the drive came from the idea that this grandmother stole his bride from him and, due to this fact, she deserved to die. In another moment, Lanzer withdrew a stone from the road imagining that the cart of his beloved could pass by there, overturn, occurring her death. Later, he put the stone in the same place.

For explaining these ambivalent movements, Freud (1909) uses the cancellation mechanism, pointing out that "compulsive acts", in two successive stages, when the second neutralizes the first, constitute a typical occurrence in the obsessional neurosis" (p. 169). Its real significance, however, lies in the fact that they are representations of a conflict between two opposing drives of approximately equal strength, such as the ambivalence between love and hate. In compulsive acts, each of the opposing trends is satisfied, in isolation; first one and then the other, although naturally an attempt is made in order to establish a certain type of logical connection between antagonistic drives.

In addition to these ambivalent drives, on this patient's medical history, although Freud (1909) has not focused in detail the identification with the father, he mentions data showing the paternal identification of Lanzer with Heirinch.

The patient's father fell in love with a poor girl before meeting the one who he married, who was a wealthy woman. The son identified with the paternal figure, falling in love for a girl also without financial resources, which put him at a crossroads, because he did not know if he would be with the beloved (poor) or with the rich woman reserved for him. As a result of this, emerges the disease that makes it impossible to finish his education and give a direction to his life. Such event Freud (1909) also interprets that occurred in the transfer; once the patient judged that Freud's family was very rich and that Freud would like to see him married with his daughter, being this the reason why he treated him well.

The patient remembered that his father and he had a very good relationship, as if they were friends, so he rejected Freud's idea that there was ambiguity of feelings regarding his father. During puberty, the patient did not have the habit of masturbation, but shortly after his father's death he went through a period in which those activities had a certain frequency, to which he was ashamed and decreased to rare occasions. Two of these occasions had in common the challenge of order and prohibition. The patient always fancied that his father was alive and in one of these fantasies consisted in studying until late and around mid-night he opened the house door, returned to the hall, took his penis out and looked at it in the mirror. Also here it is noticed an ambiguity present, since it would please his father demon-strating appreciation for the studies and he would displease him showing his genitals.

Freud (1990) then assumes that his father could have punished him for practicing masturbation when he was a child, to what the patient brings the revelation that when he was very small, he was severely beaten by his father because of a bite that he gave somebody and he showed enough aggressiveness to-wards his father, cursing him the name of objects while he was beaten. His father then interrupted the beating, amazed at the anger demonstrated by the small and commented that he would be a great man or a big criminal. According to the patient, from this time onwards, he was never beaten and became a coward for fearing to give vent to his aggressiveness.

The issue of the identification with the father emerges again in one of the conflicts presented by the young, with regard to the payment that should have been done to the Lieutenant already mentioned. His father when he was a sub officer in the army, he had a small amount of money under his responsibility and he lost this value in a card game, being helped by friend, who lent him the money to be restored. Here Freud (1909) alludes to a game of words, where the father had been acting like a 'spielratte' or a game rat. So, he felt that he owned money to the captain in reso-nance with the debt that his father might not have paid.

Apart from the paternal identification issue (and doubt), Freud (1990) provides various symbolic meanings that the issue of the rats elicited, through the patient's report. He had suffered with worms for years in his childhood, having then associated the meaning of money with the word *ratten* (rats) and *raten* (install-ments). This association with the rats also brought data from this history with his father: on one occasion, the patient saw a large animal near the tomb of his father and he judged that it was a rat, which was devouring the body of his father, what was connected to the beating he took in his childhood for biting someone.

Not only the anal eroticism arose the attention of Freud in this case, but also the strength of through that is present in this neurosis. For Freud (1990), the obsessive structures "can be classified as desires, temptations, drives, reflections, questions, orders or prohibitions" (p. 193). The obsessive thoughts suffer a similar deformation to that the oneiric thoughts pass before becoming the manifest content of a dream. The technique of obsessive thoughts deformation is the only technique of deformation by omission or ellipse. On the ellipse, he says:

> This technique preferably applies to jokes, but in the case of the Rats Man it worked well, as a means of avoiding that things were understood [...] the deformation technique by ellipse appears to be a characteristic of the obsessive neurosis; I have noticed this also in the obsessive thoughts of other patients" (Freud, 1909, p. 197).

In the obsessive neurosis, the unconscious mental processes sometimes erupt into consciousness in its pure and undeformed way. Such incursions occur at all and any stage of the thought process; and that at the moment of these incursions, the obsessive ideas can, in most case, be recognized as a long term formation. Therefore, based on the Lanzer analysis, Freud (1909) points out that the thinking in the obsessional neurosis replaces the act and instead of the substitutive act, some thought that anticipates perseveres with the compulsion full force.

According to Freud (1909), " insofar as such regression of the act to the thinking becomes more marked or less market, a case of obsessional neurosis will exhibit the obsessive thinking characteristics (i.e., obsessive ideas)" (p. 211). This means that the thought process becomes sexualized since the sexual pleasure is typically connected to the thought content "and it is seen applied to the very act of thinking, and the satisfaction derived from the fact of reaching the conclusion of a line of thought is felt as a sexual satisfaction" (Freud, 1909, p. 211-212). Thus, a thought process is obsessive or compulsive when in consequence of an inhibition on the motor end of the psychic system; it is carried out with an expenditure of energy that is normally reserved only for the actions.

Another aspect that caught the attention of Freud (1909) in the Rats Man and which can be observed in other neurotic obsessive is the manner in which these people deal with superstition. In this case, although the patient was an intelligent and cultured person, not accustomed to the most common superstitions, he believed himself being capable of having presentiments about common situations. He believed in premonitions and prophetic dreams. This way of thinking was supported on seemingly fortuitous events, like meeting a person that he had just thought, or remembering someone who he did not think for a long time and receiving news from her soon after having thought of this.

The boy realized that certain more weird feelings, in addition of not making any difference in his life, could be explained by small lapses of memory, but this did not remove the strength of such oddities in his existence. Freud (1990) rescues the childhood of this patient and points out that his mother may have helped in such peculiarity of thinking, because when he was little, it was common that his mother stated that he could not witness any events because since that day he would be sick, what actually ended up happening.

Freud (1909) then assumes that the patient wanted to have experiences like this, and even more, he reaches to the perception that the obsessive seem to need to live with the doubt, being this a way found by neurosis for attracting the sick out of reality.

According to Freud (1909) "the creation of the uncertainty is one of the methods used by neurosis in order to attract the patient out of reality and isolate him from the world" (p. 201). The doubt corresponds to the internal perception that the patient has, from his own indecision, which, as a consequence of his love inhibition through his hate, it possesses him before any intended action. Doubt is a doubt of his own love and is spreads for everything else, being able to be shifted to that which is most insignificant and worthless, leading him to the uncertainty through his protective measures. While the compulsion is an attempt for some compensation by doubt and for a correction of intolerable conditions of inhibition, of which doubt presents testimony.

For Freud (1909, the predilection of obsessive neurotic by uncertainty and by doubt leads them to guide their thoughts of preference for those themes to which the entire mankind is uncertain, being the knowledge and judgments exposed to doubt. The main topics of this nature are fatherhood, length of life and afterlife.

According to Jones (1989) "the tendency to doubt is one of the cardinal symptoms of obsessional neurosis, being the other the recurring feeling of compulsion" (p. 269). In other words, the doubt is also a fruit of ambivalence between love and hate that dominates the patient life.

Following the reasoning of the doubts and premonitory thoughts, Freud (1909) comes even more to the infantile, when he explains that behind such predictions there is a belief in the obsessive omnipotent thought. This seems to believe that his thoughts have the power to make things happen. For example, Freud told how the patient believed to have predicted the death of a man who occupied a room in which he would like to have hosted, because he was already known and because he was near a nurse with whom he had a relationship. On the occasion of a second hospitalization in order to treat his obsessions, he wanted to stay in that room and he was unable due to the occupation of this gentleman, wishing so that he could die.

When this occurred, the patient dreamed with the death of this gentleman, which marked him a lot. With this the omnipotence of his hate is configured, but of his love also appeared in the analysis, when he reports to have known a single woman, who was not young and who did not attract him; but who asked to be loved by him. The young man did not accept the attempt, and then he knew that the woman later committed suicide. Also in this case, he believed to have been able to save the woman if he had loved her.

From the richness of this clinical case, Freud (1909) emphasizes that the obsessive thinking can be classified as desires, temptations, drives, reflections, doubts, orders or prohibitions. One striking characteristic of this neurosis is the regression of the action to the thought, making the very act of thinking sexualized. These neurotic feel terror at the possibility of his thoughts becoming true in the outside world, although an important part of their mind believes in their power to do that. So, thinking about the death of someone puts that person in extreme danger.

The issue of death showed up with some regularity in the thoughts of the Rats Man, as a magical control of his part. Those who died were seen by him with sympathy and often he wished the death of other known people, in order to seem important with the condolences of those who remained alive. Freud (1909) also points out that a patient's sister died when he was from three to four years old, which in his fantasy related to his tricks.

In 1910, Lanzer married his beloved Gisela and, in 1913, he became a lawyer. Drafted by the imperial army in August 1914, he was taken prisoner by the Russians in November. He died on November 25 of the same year, without having had the time to enjoy the benefits provided by his analysis[4].

---

4 According to the report of Mahony (1991), the date of his death coincides with the date of death of his mother; since both died on November 25, 1914.

Conclusion

The analysis of the Rat Man came to open doors to the anal eroticism studies in obsessional neurosis; since we cannot forget that the report of the punishment by the rats arose the old anal eroticism of Lanzer, making the captain to take the place of his father and covering the rat with the meaning of money and debt.

From the analysis of Lanzer, the anal eroticism only came to be targeted again in the studies of Freud in 1913, in the text *The Inclination of Obsessional Neurosis*, being highlighted the anal sadistic fixation as a primary factor for the development of this neurosis in the lives of these individuals.

In addition to the anal-sadistic dynamics, I highlight that this analysis already brings two fundamental defense mechanisms for the obsessions analysis: the isolation and annulment. While in annulment we have two contradictory movements, where the first 'nulls', 'cancels' the second, the insulation does not allow that the neurotic be in contact with his desires, creating certain taboos. The analysis of this defense mechanism will be resumed, later, by Freud in 1913, when writing the text *Totem and Taboo*.

In addition to these two mechanisms, another heritage left by Freud in this case is tied to the animist thought present in obsessions. All obsessive neurotic features archaic forms of thought; as well as any act is surrounded by doubt and uncertainty due to the psychic ambivalence that is unique to this psychic structure. Such features are also resumed in 1913, in *Totem and Taboo*.

Therefore, I conclude this article with a famous phrase of Freud (1926) about obsessional neurosis: "the obsessional neurosis is, undoubtedly, the most interesting and compensatory theme of analytical research" (p. 115).

Bibliographical References

FREUD, S. (1909/1996). *Notes on a Case of Obsessional Neurosis. ESB* X. Rio de Janeiro: Imago.

_____. (1926/1996). *Inhibitions, Symptoms and Anguish. ESB*, vol. XX, Rio de Janeiro: Imago.

JONES, E. (1989). *The life and work of Sigmund Freud.* Rio de Janeiro: Imago.

MAHONY, P. (1991). *Freud and the Rats Man.* Translation of Elisabeth Saporiti and Maria da Penha Cataldi. São Paulo: Escuta.

ROUDINESCO, E.& PLON, M. (1998). *Dictionary of Psychoanalysis* Rio de Janeiro: Jorge Zahar.

The Walking Unconscious